T0146864

GBAGBONOMICS

THE INTERRUPTED PATH TO ECONOMIC INDEPENDENCE

Narcisse "Nash" Kpokou

AuthorHouse™
1663 Liberty Drive
Bloomington, IN 47403
www.authorhouse.com
Phone: 1 (800) 839-8640

Published by AuthorHouse 05/27/2015

ISBN: 978-1-5049-0848-1 (sc)
ISBN: 978-1-5049-0847-4 (e)

Library of Congress Control Number: 2015906321

Print information available on the last page.

Any people depicted in stock imagery provided by Thinkstock are models,
and such images are being used for illustrative purposes only.
Certain stock imagery © Thinkstock.

This book is printed on acid-free paper.

Because of the dynamic nature of the Internet, any web addresses or links contained in
this book may have changed since publication and may no longer be valid. The views
expressed in this work are solely those of the author and do not necessarily reflect the
views of the publisher, and the publisher hereby disclaims any responsibility for them.

CONTENTS

ACKNOWLEDGMENTS

This book would have been impossible without the genuine support and guidance of all my previous professors of economy in the United States of America. Over a year ago, I spent writing this book, I received invaluable editing support from my friends Peter Cash, Angie Beya, Christian Vabe, and my daughter Venecia Thelllin.

My biggest debt to all my children, brothers, sisters, and my lovely Mother Francoise and wonderful father Bernard, with whom I share the responsibility for joy in the most important work I will ever do.

I am greatly indebted to the United States of America for giving me the opportunity to become who I am today. I am also indebted to the many people in the international economic organizations with whom I discussed the numerous economic issues that reflect upon here.

I am also grateful to the numerous government officials in Central and East Africa for allowing me to be their Independent international Business Consultant in the USA.

Be Blessed

ABBREVIATION AND ACRONYMS

BCEAO: Banque Centrale des Etats de l' Afrique de l'Ouest

BICICI: Banque Internationale pour le commerce et l, Industrie en Cote d'ivoire

BCCI: Banque Centrale de la Cote d'ivoire

BEAC: Banque des Etats de l'afrique Centrale

CFA franc: Franc de la Communaute Financiere Africaine

CEMAC: Communaute Economic Monetaire de l 'Afrique Centrale

CEI: Commission Electorale Independente

ECOWAS: Economic Community of West African States

FPI: Front Populaire Ivoirien

EU: European Union

HIPC: Heavily Indebted Poor Countries

GDP: Gross Domestic Product

RDR: Rassemblement des Republicains

SGBCI: Societe Generale des Banques en Cote d'Ivoire

INS: Institut Nationale des Statistiques

IMF: International Monetary Fund

ICC: International Criminal Court

UN: United Nations

UEMOA: Union Economique Monetaire Ouest Africaine

PRSP: Poverty Reduction Strategy Paper

WAEMU: West African Economic and Monetary Union

INTRODUCTION

I have written this book because I saw firsthand the devastating effect of the 2010-2011 post-electoral crisis in Cote d'Ivoire. And the role played by France and the international community to overthrow President Laurent Gbagbo.

As an economist and educator, I spent a lot of time researching and thinking about the economic and social issues or impacts of the brutal shift of power caused by France. I believe it is important to view Cote d'Ivoire's Post-Electoral crisis in a dispassionate way, to put aside ideology and to look at evidences.

This book in an eye opener and is based on my professional and academic experiences in Cote d'Ivoire, Europe, and the United States. There aren't nearly as many footnotes and citations as there would be in an academic paper.

I hope "Gbagbonomics The Interrupted Path to Economic Independence" will open a worldwide debate that should occur not just behind the closed door of governments and international community.

The 2010–11 Ivorian crisis was a political crisis in Ivory Coast which began after Laurent Gbagbo, the President of Ivory Coast since 2000, was proclaimed the winner of the Ivorian election of 2010, the first election in the country in 10 years. The opposition candidate, Alassane Ouattara, and a number of countries, international organizations and world leaders claimed Ouattara had won the election. After months of attempted negotiation and sporadic violence, the crisis entered a decisive stage as

Ouattara's forces began a military offensive in which they quickly gained control of most of the country and besieged key targets in Abidjan, the country's largest city. International organizations have reported numerous human rights violations, and the UN undertook its own military action with the stated objective to protect itself and civilians. A significant step in bringing an end to the crisis occurred on 11 April 2011 upon the capture and arrest of Gbagbo in Abidjan by pro-Ouattara and French forces.

Youssouf Bakayoko, head of the Ivorian Electoral Independent Commission(CEI), announced provisional results showing that Alassane Ouattara had won the Ivorian election of 2010 in the second round with 54.1% of the vote, against 45.9% for Laurent Gbagbo; he reported that turnout was 81.09%

Paul Yao N'Dre, the President of the Constitutional Council (a body that was viewed by the opposition as favoring Gbagbo, because N'Dre was considered an ally of the President), then took to the airwaves to say that the CEI had no authority left to announce any results, because it had already missed its deadline.

Outtara said that the continuing crisis hurts the economy. As a declining economy threatens the status of Côte d'Ivoire, as the largest producer of cocoa in the world, a revival hinged on the outcome of the election

The internationally traded price for cocoa and white sugar fell in the week prior to the election on speculation that the election would spur production. On 24 January 2011, the cocoa price soared following Ouattara›s announcement that coffee and cocoa exports would be banned for a month in hope to cut off the funding for Gbagbo. Ivory Coast was also forced to default on a $2.3 billion bond as a result of the crisis.

On 9 February 2011 onwards the Abidjan stock exchange remained closed after Gbagbo›s loyalist forces invaded its offices. The following day it reopened. The regional stock exchange moved»temporarily» to Bamako, Mali after Gbagbo's troops attacked its office in Abidjan.

During the week from 14 to 18 February, four banks] had suspended their operations, and Gbagbo in response nationalized them on 17 February. Most of the cash machines in Abidjan had been empty or out of service and people rushed to the banks to withdraw their cash.

Reports suggested a cash crisis in the country due to a lack of capital inflows and runs on banks forcing national financial institutions to also deplete their reserves. Several banks ceased operations in the country. The move led to Gbagbo loyalist forces to have "nationalized" those banks and "requisitioned" cash from the Central Bank's Abidjan bureau.

In 2010, the authorities pursued implementation of the 2009-11 financial and economic program the PRSP, which should result in the completion point in the Heavily Indebted Poor Countries (HIPC) Initiative being reached during the first half of 2011. This program aims to achieve macroeconomic stability, create conditions for sustained growth and a fair share-out of its fruits, and to fight poverty more efficiently through tighter management of public finances and the construction of economic and social infrastructures.

These forecasts were based on expectations of relatively low receipts from direct taxes, notably taxes on industrial and commercial profits, resulting from lower activity levels in the secondary and tertiary sectors. Tax exemptions granted to take the crisis into account should contribute to this reduction. It should be noted that value added tax (VAT) on hotels and tourism is expected to be reduced in 2011 as a means of mitigating the effects of the crisis in these sectors. Expenditure and net lending represented 21.7% of GDP in 2010, slightly more than the 21.1% figure registered in 2009. Of its two main components, current expenditure rose from 17.9% in 2009 to 18.3% in 2010, while capital expenditure edged up from 3.1% of GDP to 3.2%. As regards current expenditure, the public sector wage bill, which rose from 6.8% of GDP in 2009 to 6.9% in 2010, was relatively well controlled, taking account of the 7.2% of GDP limit set by the 2010 economic program agreed with the International Monetary Fund (IMF). However, the ratio of the public sector wage bill to fiscal revenue stagnated at 41.5% as in 2009, slightly below the 41.3% level fixed by the 2010 economic program. Capital expenditure came out at 3.2%

of GDP compared with 3.1% in 2009, the slight increase coming from spending on the construction and rehabilitation of basic socio-economic infrastructures. Overall, budget execution in 2010 was marked by a small increase in revenues and grants.

Despite these reforms, efforts to mobilize internal resources in Côte d'Ivoire are still faced with major revenue shortfalls. According to the government tax department (DGI), tax reductions granted by the state to the private sector between 2000 and 2010 amounted to more than 800 billion CFA franc, or an average of 80 billion CFA franc per year. in the 2011 budget. A methodological explanation of the guidelines was in preparation as a means of facilitating definition of the budgetary attributions of other ministries. Debt servicing in 2010 was set at 542.2 billion CFA franc, of which 316.8 billion CFA franc was for external debt according to AFDB, OECD, UNDP, UNECA African Economic Outlook 2010

One of the most important influences in the economic and political life of African states which were formerly French colonies is the impact of a common currency; the Communuate Financiere de l'Afrique ('CFA') franc. There are actually two separate CFA francs in circulation. The first is that of the West African Economic and Monetary Union (WAEMU) which comprises eight West African countries (Benin, Burkina Faso, Guinea-Bissau, Ivory Coast, Mali, Niger, Senegal and Togo. The second is that of the Central African Economic and Monetary Community (CEMAC) which comprises six Central African countries (Cameroon, Central African Republic, Chad, Congo-Brazzaville, Equatorial Guinea and Gabon). This division corresponds to the pre-colonial AOF (Afrique Occidentale Française) and the AEF (Afrique Équatoriale Française), with the exception that Guinea-Bissau was formerly Portuguese and Equatorial Guinea Spanish).

Each of these two groups issues its own CFA franc. The WAEMU CFA franc is issued by the BCEAO (Banque Centrale des Etats de l'Afrique de l'Ouest) and the CEMAC CFA franc is issued by the BEAC (Banque des Etats de l'Afrique Centrale).

The monetary policy governing such a diverse aggregation of countries is uncomplicated because it is, in fact, operated by the French Treasury, without reference to the central fiscal authorities of any of the WAEMU or the CEMAC. Under the terms of the agreement which set up these banks and the CFA the Central Bank of each African country is obliged to keep at least 65% of its foreign exchange reserves in an *"operations account"* held at the French Treasury, as well as another 20% to cover financial liabilities.

The CFA central banks also impose a cap on credit extended to each member country equivalent to 20% of that country's public revenue in the preceding year. Even though the BEAC and the BCEAO have an overdraft facility with the French Treasury, the drawdowns on those overdraft facilities are subject to the consent of the French Treasury. The final say is that of the French Treasury which has invested the foreign reserves of the African countries in its own name on the Paris Bourse.

In short, more than 80% of the foreign reserves of these African countries are deposited in the *"operations accounts"* controlled by the French Treasury. The two CFA banks are African in name, but have no monetary policies of their own. The countries themselves do not know, nor are they told, how much of the pool of foreign reserves held by the French Treasury belongs to them as a group or individually.

The earnings of the investment of these funds in the French Treasury pool are supposed to be added to the pool but no accounting is given to either the banks or the countries of the details of any such changes. The limited group of high officials in the French Treasury who have knowledge of the amounts in the *"operations accounts"*, where these funds are invested; whether there is a profit on these investments; are prohibited from disclosing any of this information to the CFA banks or the central banks of the African states.

This makes it impossible for African members to regulate their own monetary policies. The most inefficient and wasteful countries are able to use the foreign reserves of the more prudent countries without any meaningful intervention by the wealthier and more successful countries. The fact that as the French GDP grows and the parity of the Euro to the dollar (the main currency of international trade) appreciates there is the constant danger that the CFA franc may be fixed at too high an exchange rate. This dampens the growth in trade between Africa and the rest of the world and allows other countries, especially in Asia, to use their more flexible exchange rates to gain market share, supplanting the Africans.

The creation and maintenance of the French domination of the francophone African economies is the product of a long period of French colonialism and the learned dependence of the African states. *France wishes that no UEMOA countries be truly sovereign and self-sufficient, and thus able to escape their control. And the crucial point to prevent that Cote d'Ivoire is controlled by France is the issuance of a national currency. No country could claim to be sovereign if it does not issue its owns currency, interest-free and debt free.* The creation of a national currency is the key to the development of an economy. The Member States of the UEMOA in particular Cote d'Ivoire cannot be independent because they are caught up in the CFA franc and the French Treasury.

I hope my book will open a debate, a debate that should not occur just behind the closed doors of governments and international organizations. This book should provide more information about the 50 years of France in Cote d'Ivoire.

More information will lead to better policies, economic independence and better results. If that happens, then I feel I have made a contribution.

CHAPTER 1

POST-ELECTION CONFLICT AND THE FALL OF GBAGBO

After six years of postponement, the Ivorian presidential election takes place in the context of a divided country. During the election campaign, the beginnings of future tensions are palpable. The first round, held on 31 October 2010, bears the traces. But it is in the second round on 28 November, which pits incumbent President Laurent Gbagbo to the former prime minister Alassane Ouattara, as the situation deteriorates.

Waiting for results of the vote plunged the country into confusion, as shown in this incident: November 30, two days after the election, Gbagbo's representatives in the electoral commission prevented the announcement of partial results in Abidjan. This tension within the commission delayed the announcement of results.

A first verdict gives proclaimed by the Independent Electoral Commission gives the challenger Ouattara the winner with 54.1% of votes. These results are immediately invalidated by the Constitutional Council. The Council believes that the figures, which were announced after the expiry of the three-day period provided by the electoral code, are zero. The next day, the Constitutional Council declared Gbagbo president.

The two men then claiming their separate victory. On 4 December, Laurent Gbagbo is investing president and his sworn opponent "as President of the Republic." and appointed Gilbert Aké as prime minister

The United States, France and Britain recognized the victory of Ouattara. ECOWAS suspends Ivory Coast. UN calls for respect of the results announced by the Independent Electoral Commission, on pain of sanctions. Even Russia, after several days of hesitation, adopts the Declaration of the UN Security Council. And the African Union (AU) suspended Ivory Coast before President of the African Union Commission, Jean Ping, presents Laurent Gbagbo a letter asking him to step down.

The European Union (EU) called the Ivorian army to place themselves under the authority of Ouattara and French President Nicolas Sarkozy issued an ultimatum to Gbagbo: it requires leaving before the end of the week, as pain of being hit by EU sanctions

President of the World Bank announced that loans to Ivory Coast were frozen. More importantly, the next day, seven finance ministers of the West African Economic and Monetary Union (WAEMU) asked the Central Bank of West African States (BCEAO) to allow only representatives of the Ivorian president "legitimately elected," Alassane Ouattara, to manage the accounts of the country.

Alassane Ouattara ordered the arrest of cocoa exports whose country is the first world producer, hoping to financially strangle Gbagbo. In response, Laurent Gbagbo takes control of the purchase and export of cocoa.

Gbagbo "requisition" in Côte d'Ivoire agencies of the BCEAO, but Ouattara announces their "closure". These strategies of suffocation eventually block the financial system.

While international pressure on Gbagbo increases meanwhile, the African Union asked the Kenyan Prime Minister Raila Odinga to try to resolve the political crisis, and then sets up a "panel" of heads of state on the crisis. Several shuttles ECOWAS and AU succeed in Abidjan in vain. Finally, on March 31, the Security Council of the United Nations vote unanimously Resolution 1975, which urges Laurent Gbagbo to step down and submit to the outgoing president and his family to sanctions.

large-scale massacres were committed in Duékoué between 27 and 29 March, the date of the conquest by the Ouattara of this city from the west. The doubts relate to the balance sheet from 300 to a 1000 deaths.

The former northern rebels allied with Alassane Ouattara created the Republican Forces of Côte d'Ivoire (FRCI), composed of soldiers who defected SDS and former rebel New Forces.

After the pro-Gbagbo forces were able to regain ground in Abidjan from April 8, taking control of several neighborhoods, the French forces Licorne and UNOCI launched a strike campaign on the bastions of the President Gbagbo.

On April 11, in the early afternoon, Laurent Gbagbo was arrested by the French and the U.N taken to the Golf Hotel, Ouattara camp HQ in Abidjan.

Gbagbo remains the flame that will enlighten young African generations in search of the liberation of Africa must fully enjoy the riches, God's gift and the vultures of international finance come and steal while diving in African misery.

An unprecedented disinformation campaign is being orchestrated to justify and replace Gbagbo with Ouattara totally devoted to the interests of multinationals.

Ouattara is a former Deputy CEO of the IMF, and a former Prime Minister of Houphouet Boigny who in 1990 administered the Ivorian people into a profound social and economic distress.

He is the puppet nominated by the major power to lead the Ivory Coast and to ensure that their interest are not threatened by the presence of uncompromising and patriotic men such as Laurent Gbagbo a longtime opponent of Houphouet (1970-1990s).

French and the imperialists' power have agreed to remove Gbagbo who is guilty of pursuing a national power a national policy prejudicial to their profits

The war perpetrator in chief who cannot forgive Gbagbo for opening the oil markets to American companies in 2002. It was a crime to have opened the preserve of French capitalists to others.

Another intolerable offense was that Gbagbo dared to open the road leading to oil in the Gulf of Guinea to emerging rivals such as China and Russia. To inflict deserved correction, Sarkozy has rallied to the U S to crush the recidivist offender and in the process any eventual nationalist leader that would dare frolic with "their oil reserves and minerals".

50 years after the country formal independence was achieved without struggle and sacrifice. Beyond the Ivory Coast, the neo-colonialists are most afraid that this resistance spread to former French colonies and that "La Francafrique "is led to affirm its desire for true independence beginning with the denunciation of the puppets of the great French bourgeoisie.

The slogan "respect the democratic choice of the people" is a mockery coming from the leaders of the imperialists powers which have orchestrated, covered and sustained cruel dictatorships around the world as long as their capitalists businesses.

In all cases, although Gbagbo has close links with the French Socialists, who have shown their zeal to defend the neo-colonialist, even if his past alliances allow small casts of doubt on the objectives he defends; the struggle that ensued between the imperialists powers and the greatmass of the Ivorian people, appalled by the arrogance of the former still opt to no longer tolerate the denomination and exploitation they have endured for decades.

As I mentioned earlier Gbagbo was championing the cause of Ivorian economic emancipation and African liberation by challenging the status quo suffered by Francophone nations since their independence and Ouattara was seen to be protecting French interests given his background.

The statute quo allowed France to take up to 80% of the revenue from Francophone countries back to Paris to build French economy at the expense of Francophone states. This diabolic arrangement was made in the 1960s when these states were fighting for their independence from the French.

Gbagbo was aware of this repugnant arrangement and when he became president in 2000 began to challenge this arrangement by giving some government contracts to Chinese firms rather than French companies who had previously secured all government contracts, by restricting the market share of French companies in Ivory Coast who previously enjoyed a total monopoly of the Ivorian market and by refusing to pay the French government royalties to use his own presidential palace and other institutions.

The French political elites who knew of Gbagbo's Pan African vision, were determined to use every means necessary to stop Gbagbo on his track. The French intensified their attacks on Gbagbo's rule by imposing economic sanctions and making it difficult for Ivory Coast to generate income through its main export cocoa.

However the elections in 2010 were an opportune moment for the French to execute their plan. This plan entailed supporting their anointed son Ouattara to the hilt by manipulating the voter register in Ouattara strongholds in the north of the country and also having strong influence of the electoral commission.

Therefore these acts show that the French were determined to get rid of Gbagbo by any means necessary because as a result of his Panafrican vision he was seen as a serious threat to France's economic interest in Africa.

This heinous act itself sets a very bad precedent, because if an African leader in a former French colony decides to step out of the colonial arrangement, which is not grossly unfair but racist, then that leader can expect to be taken out by the French military which is absolutely despicable and in this supposedly democratic age is totally unacceptable. It is interesting to note that those African leaders who serve French interests have stayed in power for a long time despite committing gross human rights abuses.

CHAPTER 2

ECONOMIC POLICY OF GBAGBO

Upon his arrival in power Gbaggo gives a huge swing to the left, which contrast with the African aristocratic vision of the founding father. The former President Houphouet Boigny.

The main economics idea of Gbagbo was called the refoundation. This economic concept was the cornerstone of his political and economic program. He intended to use the refoundation to boost international relations to promote a win –win partnership with foreign investors and businesses.

The first project aims to reform agriculture field which represent over 40% of the GDP. Gbagbo attacks the wealthiest people linked to French system. The democratization of education through the establishment of new education opens to the lower class.

Gbagbo strongly believes that the administration and the public service is the key of social contract between government and the people. According to him, public service should served the people not the people to serve the public service.

In addition, he allowed access the administration and the army to the lower sons and daughter of the middle, and the working classes.

He viewed democracy, liberty, and adopt decentralization to reduce inequalities among the various regions of Cote d'ivoire. Gbagbo wanted to build a strong civil society, and strengthen all the institutions in other to have a modern country.

His main concern was to place Ivorian at the center of any economic activities in other to promote businesses, industrial activities, and financial institutions.

Gbagbo a believer of Trickle Down Economy. Because he thinks that a tax break to businesses will benefit to lower class, and will boost the entire economy.

The concept of social business was highly appreciated by Gbagbo, and he made it one of the key concepts in the Gbagbonomics. He mentioned it in one of his speech saying that the aim is not just to create job and empower young people- but also to generate income and develop an entrepreneurial culture for the poor and worst vulnerable people.

Over 10 years Gbagbo has demonstrated that any African nation can do a better job, and implement a self reliance policy. The growth rate was negative in 2000. This growth rate increases and growing since 2006. According to the IMF The GDP growth has been maintained continuously from 2004 to 2009, and the rate of economic growth has been positive (1.6% in 2004, 1.8% in 2005, 1,2% in 2006, 1,5% in 2007, 2.3% in 2008, 3.8% in 2009.

Nominal GDP has continuously increased. It went from 7, 630 billion FCFA in 2000 to 10486 500 000 000 FCFA in 2008 has amounted to 10,925 billion F CFA in 2009, will become 11,000 billion FCFA in 2010; it is an economic certainty bill

Tax revenues are very large increase (1.0354 trillion in 2000 -1 795.6 billion in 2009, representing an increase of 73.42% despite the cost of 800 billion CFA francs, of all dropouts tax revenues taken in response to the crisis, and without the tax burden have increased on average for almost 15 years. The performance is due to the widening of the tax base and reforms put in place since 2000 with Gbagbo governance, including computerization and the standard bill.

The fiscal deficit is low and stands at 162.5 billion CFA Francs in 2009 or 1.5% of GDP. This rate is well below the EU rate 3%. Under Gbagbo leadership the fixed budget was funded 92% by the resources of Cote d'Ivoire.

The state budget has been growing since 2001 from 1 289 billion FCFA in 2001, it increased to 2 529 billion FCFA in 2009, an increase of 96%. Government revenues account for 92% of the state budget. Until 2000, they accounted for an average of 84% of the state budget. Fiscal discipline imposed by the "Safe Budget" has led to a surplus of 69.8 billion

The domestic debt arrears are lower in 2009. They amounted to 132 billion in times of crisis and the state since 2000, pays on average to domestic creditors under domestic debt 237 820 000 000 FCFA per year (1).

According to the World Bank the stock of external debt has declined sharply with the HIPC. He passed 6,700 billion FCFA in 2000 to 4,000 billion FCFA (including cancelation already obtained) recently in 2009, a decrease of 40, 2% and the ration of external debt to GDP ratio was about 16.6% (2).

Industrial production has increased since 2000. The overall index of production was 7.8% in 2000 increased to 4.8% in 2000, either an increase of 12.6% between 2000 and 2009 (14).

Export raised in value. The spend 2.572 billion in 2000 to 4,846 billion CFA francs; the trade balance grew rapidly, it went from 802.5 billion in 2000(3).

Investment increased 207 billion CFA franc in 2000, they rose to 335.2 billion CFA francs. Note that as the Ivory Coast had more wealth Gbagbo favored investments for its governance (2.7% of GDP in 2000 to 3.06% in 2009 (4).

Inflation under Gbagbo's governance has decreased. The inflation rate was 1% in 2009 against 2.5% in 2000, this rate of 1% during the rule of

Gbagbo is well below the rate of inflation in the WAEMU community standard which is 3% recommended.

Credit to the economy (finance domestic economy activity) has seen tremendous growth during the rule of Laurent Gbagbo. This outstanding increased from 39.3 billion in 2000 to 2 477 billions in 2009 (5).

The money supply has more doubled between 2000 and 2009 during the rule of Gbagbo. It went from 1570,3 milliards in 2000 to 3525,5 milliards in 2009. The balance of foreign assets which was in deficit before 2000 became largely positive in 2009.

Cote d' Ivoire from the point of its external financial correspondent has been increasingly credible and reliable with the governance of Laurent Gbagbo.

Under Gbagbo, from the point of view of socio-economic infrastructure, there is an extension of the high north to Yamoussoukro, the improved road Adzope –Abidjan, paving the axis Odienne - Tingrelela (rebel Zone) under the supervision and implementation of the Road Management Agency (AGEROUTE) and the Road Maintenance Fund (IRON).

Yards and roads works and urban development around the urban infrastructure Emergency Program (PUIR) by President Laurent Gbagbo in 2008 with funding from the World Bank. The section between the junction of the Zoo and Samake in Abobo.

Widening the road linking the crossroads of Williams to the Zoo, a distance of 2,2 Km, the asphalting of the road 2 Km long. Extending from the side of Andre Malraux, rebuilding the interchange Gesco Highway North Road Dabou exchanger (new pedestrian bridge) to Bracodi- Williamsvillle, coupled with the development of the Guru Bassin Adjame from exchanger Agban, the new castle Abbata water district Bingerville treating several critical points in Yopougon and Niangoin Sideci and Rivera (and the two –lane bridge Bouafle on the road section Bouafle-Daloa, cleaning out gutters, urban sanitation the garbage collection in the city of Abidjan and repairs tarred road throughout the country (6).

In conclusion, all the respective values of the above indicators show that governance of Laurent Gbagbo was more beneficial to the economy of Cote d'Ivoire. The evidence of success has been the concept of secure budget set up by Bohouan Bouabre minister in the Gbagbo regime.

The International Monetary Fund (IMF), stated that the economic efforts of the Ouattara's government marks a point of honor of exceptional work done by Cote d'Ivoire in recent years.

Indeed, after the reforms in the Ministry of Economy and Finance from 2001 including the concept of a fixed budget set up by Bohoun Bouabre Minister in the Gbagbo regime, Cote d'ivoire saw its budget increase each year due to strict management of state resources.

This budget is so called "secure" in that it takes into account "the cash that we are certain to cover" expenses and prioritized, said Minister of Finance, Bohoun Bouabre. The budget thus integrates any external support, while the government is trying to reconnect with international donors to discuss a possible resumption of their aid suspended since 1999.

The government expect 1070.7 billion CFA in tax revenue, 83 billion CFA additional domestic resources and external resources 130.3 billion. On spending, the service of the public debt absorbs 292.8 billion, of which 251.9 billion in foreign debt, 731.2 billion for recurrent expenditures and 260.8 billion of capital expenditure.

This budget discipline now includes remediation spending and state revenues. Budget passed gradually from 1289.1 to 2529.5 billion in 2009 to 3.16 trillion in 2012. The challenge remains for Cote d'Ivoire the principles of good governances. Continuing reforms, strengthening control and the fight against corruption.

Some fiscal orthodoxy is required, the springs are now measured in numbers in all sectors and the financial authorities of the state with very few non sequenced expenditures (Denos). What makes Cote d'Ivoire one of the best students of Bretton Woods, mainly the IMF.

Since then, Cote d' Ivoire which meanwhile has fully returned to the international financial community. Ouattara's government has kept the philosophy of secure budget by adapting it to new contingencies. And despite the post –election crisis that severely affected the economics of the state, Cote d'Ivoire held its course. Managing to maintain the standard of living of workers, to ensure the payment of salaries of civil servants despite the weight of ambient unemployment and social problems.

The war imposed by France had contributed to the country's division. South controlled by President Gbagbo and the north by the rebellion of Ouattara.

During the first four years of the war, economic growth was negative with -0.4% largely less than that of the WAEMU member countries was 4.1% and as sub-Saharan Africa, which was 4, 9%. Many companies run by non-nationals have been abandoned.

Similarly, foreign direct investment (FDI) had declined. This reduction has increased unemployment in the country, the rate was already high before 2000. And it struck more young people.

The financial sector was also hit hard because of closure of all CNO zone bank branches. Despite this precarious situation, President Gbagbo had made great efforts to freeze the country's internal crisis. He undertook the recovery of the Ivorian economy by getting in 2010 an inflation rate of 6.5% under control and the positive rate growth: 1.6% in 2004, 1.8% in 2005 and 3, 7% in 2010, which remain above the level of the natural growth rate of the Ivorian population estimated 3.3%.

Agriculture, livestock and fishing occupied in 2009 66% of the workforce and contributing 70% of export earnings.

Agriculture expresses its primacy in the economic activity of the Ivory Coast. This agriculture is characterized by the domination of the couple -cacao coffee accounting for 40% of export earnings and 20% of GDP and supports 7 million Ivorian

Ivory Coast produces 40% of cocoa world production, remains the country's main economic resource. Under the authority of President Gbagbo, Cote d'Ivoire has occupied the top spot globally 1.4 billion cocoa Tons (year 2008-2009) and is among the top ten coffee producers.

President Gbagbo encouraged the development of other production sectors for export. During his tenure at the head of the country, the average annual production was: palm oil 105.000 T, cotton 180.000T, 142.000T rubber, bananas 307.000T, 226.000T pineapple, palm kernel 980,000T, cashew nuts 210 T.

In 2000 President Gbagbo had placed particular emphasis on the development of livestock to reduce the import of livestock. According to the Department of Animal Production the national cattle herd was composed of (1 million) of small ruminants has little meadows (3 million) goats, sheep, pigs (300,000 t) and (28 million) of poultry.

Gbagbo had developed fishing, and concluded cooperation agreements with the European Union and Guinea Bissau.

To help the industry Ivorian President Gbagbo had introduced the legal level, fiscal reforms, budgetary, and had strengthened regulations related to public markets for a more competitive Ivorian industry.

From 2002 to 2010, oil extraction and mining had increased by 79% and the management of resources from the oil sector was published by the Ivorian government. Chemical industries had increased by 10.5% in 2010 despite the Ivory Coast was divided into two.

The tertiary services represented 54% of GDP in 2005. However this sector was the most affected by the crisis that began in 2002. According to the Ministry of Commerce, the sector recorded a decline of 5% of the overall activity of the companies' services.

To stimulate economic develop, President Gbagbo ordered the financial participation of the state in the specialized banks. These specialized financial institutions had encouraged investment and supported the agricultural sector, the acquisition of consumer goods, and creating jobs.

Gbagbo asked his government to adapt the Ivorian tax the context of the political and military crisis. This crisis had led to a sharp drop in foreign direct investment (FDI), a drastic reduction many businesses and corporations has abandoned pending a final resolution of the crisis.

In this context, President Gbagbo has taken specific measures of tax relief and remediation financial statements. Operationally this reform was accompanied by the integrated management system of public finances (SIGFIP). This is a totally computerized approach having as vocation, improve the preparation of operating budgets and investments.

To avoid dependence of France, President Gbagbo had created specialized banks (The Bank for financing agriculture (BFA), Bank of habitat Ivory Coast (BHCI) and the National Bank of investment (BNI) created partly in response to the management of deposits of the sinking fund CAA), who collaborated with banks to private and foreign capital.

The World Bank and the IMF had acknowledged that the government of President Gbagbo had made a good job in his effort of structural reforms and its production of better strategic documents for poverty reduction (PRSP).

Mr Madani Tall, Operations Directors of the World Bank for the Ivory Coast stated "We are pleased that President Gbagbo and his government have reached the decision point under the Heavily Indebted Poor Countries HIPC".

Although the Ivory Coast was divided into two, the Ivorian economy had shown signs of vitality and diversification by improving the business environment. So hearing that President Gbagbo has used taxpayer money to stay in power, it is loss of words and it is senseless.

President Ouattara promised billions of CFA franc Ivorian. He even said to outperform the Gbagbo. Everywhere we saw commercials "ADO Solution". Already 4 in power years, it is a disaster.

No macroeconomic indicator is rising, as long as the Ivory Coast is not divided as during the tenure of Gbagbo. Ouattara brought killing, insecurity, tribalism, humiliation, intimidation, and rape.

Ivorian of all political parties are saying "everything is going wrong in Cote d'Ivoire every year since Ouattara is in power". Widely reported in the media, discomfort inflames public opinion.

CHAPTER 3

COTE D'IVOIRE: HIGHLY INDEBTED POOR COUNTRY "HIPC"

Since the year 2002, the Ivory Coast is in a state of neither peace nor war with governments "Nsasa" that succeeded with the first minister imposed by Françafrique and the international community.

Cote d'ivoire long sociopolitical crisis weakened its economy and adversely affected the population's standard of living. Indeed, according to the 2008 household standard of living survey, 48.9 percent of the population lives in poverty nationwide (compared to 38.2 percent in 2002) and 62.5 percent in rural areas.

The country's ranking in the UN Human Development Index (HDI) deteriorated from 154th in 199 to 166 in 2007. Since the late 1990s, the gross primary school enrollment stagnated at about 70 percent, mortality rates of children under 5 increased from 175 to 195 per thousand and life expectancy at birth declined from 49 in 1995 to 47 in 2006. Basic public social services have been seriously degraded, especially in the Center, North, and West of the country.

Cote d' Ivoire who had returned to financial institutions saw the government program of the party in power abruptly interrupted by a coup that failed and turned into rebellion supported by some of the Ivorian political dinosaurs. After several agreements, the Ivorian opposition backed by the rebels accept important positions in the government formed from

Paris with the sole aim to derail the ambitious government program of President Gbagbo.

Despite the vicious attack against Cote d'Ivoire major projects and investments were stopped, President Gbagbo continued to honor its commitments vis a vis to financial institutions by paying interest on debt services. While the coffers of the state are not entirely unified, the government of President Gbagbo has made a considerable effort, and has implemented few structural reforms supported by the IMF and the World Bank.

COTE D'IVOIRE'S EXTERNAL DEBTS AND THE NEW DEAL WITH IMF AND THE WORLD BANK

It is important to remember that it's been twenty years since Cote d'Ivoire ran after the short program to offer him a debt relief 7000 billion FCFA contracted by governments of the 70, 80 and 90. The government of Gbagbo program should be supported by the IMF and the World Bank. He has also produced the Strategy Document for Poverty Reduction (PRSP) who clearly served as bridgehead at its input to the decision point under the HIPC initiative.

Mr John Lipsky, Deputy Managing Director of the IMF, said: 'Cote d'ivoire has fulfilled the conditions to reach the decision point under the enhanced HIPC Initiative.

To reach the completion point, Côte d'Ivoire will achieve satisfactory performance implement the strategy of poverty reduction for at Least one year, apply the proposed measures, including structural and social reforms, including the areas of management of public finance, debt management and governance'

Mr Arend Kouwenaar, IMF mission chief in Cote d'Ivoire, said: "After more than a decade of civil strife and economic difficulties, Cote d'ivoire has embarked on the path of economic recovery and political normalization. Despite the negative impact of the slowdown in the global economy, the results achieved under the IMF-supported programs have been generally satisfactory.

Mr Madani Tall, Director of Operations of the World Bank for Cote d'ivoire said: "We are pleased that President Gbagbo and his government reached the decision point under the HIPC Initiative.

The country should rapidly meet the conditions that will allow him to cross the completion point and thus to benefit from the full debt relief. It will free up resources to fund critical spending on social sectors.

President Gbagbo was determined to improve governance, to promote transparency in the management of public finances and debt, accelerate reforms in the areas of energy, coffee / cocoa, and strengthen social programs in accordance with the triggers defined in the context of the completion point. The implementation of these reforms is vital to accelerate growth and increase living standards."

"The first challenge we have noted with this financial support, is the proper use and I will ensure that this is done in the rigor and transparency. I attach the price," to declare Gbagbo, on national television, as a result of the funding agreement with the International Monetary Fund (IMF)."

The IMF representative in Cote d'Ivoire has announced that the program will get the government to shift its focus towards expenditure poverty reduction and accelerated growth. This implies that the New Deal of the Ivorian government is to invest in profusion in education, health, economic infrastructure and in the macro and micro -projects that will allow Ivorian to fight the global food crisis. Today 'Map Road' government remains clear; every Ivorian who has a good sense and is not blinded by hatred can conscientiously give reason to President Gbagbo when he began to arrest his most unscrupulous close to unchain the MACA.

The World Bank and IMF acknowledged that the Gbagbo government has done a good job carrying out structural reforms and producing a strategic document for poverty reduction (PRSP).

The events of April 11 has changed the political dynamics in Cote d'ivoire with the arrival of Ouattara in power. The government of President Ouattara Senior Economist should clearly address poverty, increase growth and find solutions to social conflicts and especially reconcile all Ivorian. Also the billions that will be immediately available for Ivory Coast to be used to send a strong signal to Ivorian who have not quit sacrifices since the beginning of the crisis.

Today 34 countries benefiting from the HIPC initiative and the payment under the debt service has on average decreased by 2% of GDP between 2002 and 2007. The government of Ouattara must understand that debt reduction will have a tangible impact on poverty if and only if the freed resources are targeted on the most impoverished sections of the population

STRUCTURAL REFORM AND GOOD GOVERNANCE

Before Cote d' Ivoire is considered HIPC devoting a little more of our resources to debt service that social service. We need the government of Ouattara draws successful models of some countries that enjoys the benefits of the HIPC.

For example, Tanzania remains a model to follow. These countries have increased their spending on health, education and infrastructure which average six times the amount of payments of debt service.

The IMF representative in Côte d'Ivoire has also highlighted the existence of a special account to finance investments. I fully agree that this fund be set up to help and encourage youth and create projects that can reduce the food crisis deficit. Better, the transformation of our raw materials and our agricultural products must occupy a prominent place in the new economic policy.

The benefit of being classified as HIPC must allow Cote d'ivoire to enter the real industrialization phase so that we can add value to our industry and reduce poverty. Being a supporter of "Trickle Down Economy Theory"

(This is the trickling down of wealth, the more the rich get richer the poor benefit more in).

To be clearer, the investment-tax credit stimulate enterprises to invest given that they are in business to make profits, and have learned to do so, so that spending, production and employment increase, thus Record will benefits to the unemployed, children and poor women.

I believe that a review of tax policy should be considered to encourage growth, mastering inflation and reduce unemployment that is the cause of poverty and improve the delivery of basic services.

No doubt to succeed Cote d'ivoire must strengthen its economic policy and encourage Ivorian to join hands around a new contract that requires real reconciliation for sustainable development. Cote d'Ivoire's decision point and eligibility for the HIPC Initiative assistance was one of the primary focus for President Gbagbo to eradicate poverty and work for a sustainable development and to give resources to small businesses to create jobs.

Gbagbo pointed out that "The causes of increasing poverty in Cote d'Ivoire are to found in the deep inequality."

The Ivory Coast is a country with some of the largest reserves of strategic raw materials in the world, cheap energy sources, optimal opportunities for agricultural and livestock production, huge tourist attractions and a very good location in terms of economic geography. However, more than 80% of its 20 million are poor and more than two thirds of young Ivorian are unemployed.

For example, it should be noted that between 2010 and 2013, the number of poor has raised 18 million and their percentage is increasing under Ouattara's leaderships

First, it must be stressed that about 8% richest of the Ivorian population receive 60% of the national Ivorian income and the poorest 92% receive only 40% of this income.

In access to productive assets such as land. Considerable rural population does not access the most basic good of production. There are inequalities in education, because the richest 10% have a minimum of twelve years of schooling, while 90% with the lowest incomes barely reach five years of schooling. This results in lower wages, because the gap between the skilled and unskilled labor is one of the largest.

There are great inequalities in health, due to the lower life expectancy and maternal and infant mortality. 2013 of 2010 of diseases associated with poverty have caused the death of 2,600 children in Ivory Coast.

Poverty would be half compared to that which currently exists if Gbagbo's government program had been applied. The increase in inequality has doubled poverty. This is what I call poverty "unnecessary", which is caused only more inequality.

There are small and medium enterprises in the Ivory Coast, which are the main source of employment and that can generate a lot more, but receive only 5% of the total volume of loans granted by the colonial banks in Cote d ivory.

Ouattara regime must address the eradication of poverty because the HIPC completion point is a major asset for poverty reduction. The clamor on inequality and poverty extends, because Ouattara is not interested in the Ivorian daily life from all regions and all political parties.

Brazil's Zero Hunger program, for example, is absolutely anti-inequality and develops an original strategy seeking to include the entire society and not just the state in working to facilitate the fundamental human right to food.

It should thoroughly discuss the problem of poverty and development. These are not magical keys, but any comparison between more or less unequal societies shows the importance of trust and confidence within a company's ability to associate, civic consciousness and values ethical.

Remittances from Ivorian immigrants from Europe, North America, Africa, and the Middle East to help those who stayed in the Ivory Coast, accounted for less than 3 billion CFA in 2012 resource flows did not enter into the calculations of traditional economists, and it is a kind of perfect capital, which does not generate foreign debt, but go to the areas that are most in social needs and have an important multiplier effect.

Ouattara a former senior economist of the World Bank and IMF should ultimately put the economy at the service of ethical values such as the right of families and children, or the young people to have a job or older people to be protected. 70% of people over sixty years in Ivory Coast have no resource. It must be an ethical responsibility in public policy and in the activities of private companies and political party that want to lead the future of Cote d'ivoire should follow this model.

It is important to mention that corruption still consumes up to 10% of the Ivorian gross domestic. To fight against corruption the strategy of the legislature of the southern Brazilian state of Rio Grande do Sul, which orders that the current economic budget is accompanied with a social budget with measurable goals must be adopted and published every year.

DEBTS AND ECONOMIC GROWTH

Adama Koné, General Director of Treasury and Public Accounting launched May 30, 2013, the fourth compulsory loan in the financial market of the WAEMU bonds of 93 billion CFA franc, the loan is paid at an interest rate of 6.00% net of tax.

He pointed out that "Ivory Coast is growing, evidenced by the sites and major development programs and ongoing restructuring.

Bonds are a common form of investment financing. Its advantages presented by the director of the treasury and taken up by the press, are admissible. But they cannot be relevant if at the same time, some of the reservations that this option was presented.

The state of Ivory Coast borrows for a specific purpose. The funds must have a destination that the system should allow. In a more demanding environment, where a credit line is opened, the funds are released gradually as the planned projects are implemented and validated. In this case, the only authority that can control the allocation of these funds is the parliament. But in Ivory Coast, the parliament is a sounding board of executive power. The power of parliament as a controller of budget execution has not been demonstrated to be polite!

By this direct appeal to the public savings, the Ivorian authorities escape the conditions imposed by donors when giving their contest. These include transparency, good management, discipline, etc. But these constraints involved in the establishment of the rules of good governance, democracy and the end of economic prosperity.

The funds collected by the Ivorian public authorities are quite high and can only fail if the government plays the role of the private operators whose main purpose is to facilitate the economic game. The main function of private agents is to create wealth and those of the state, to ensure the proper functioning of the system. Local savings, especially in a country such as Ivory Coast, is therefore intended to be used to finance the private sector simply because the state has other means to raise funds to finance development projects.

Government bonds are risk-free securities (or negligible risk). Therefore, they are the basis for assessing the risk premium. To attract capital, the government offers relatively high interest rate. Consequently, risky operations, if we take into account the risk premium, the requirement for operators in terms of return on investment can be than high. If a title earn 7% or even 5% risk how should be a stake in a company of the place, for example?

The culture of debate must move to Cote d'Ivoire. The debate should be open and democratic especially when it comes to debt. The consequences on the whole economy are significant. It remains true that the call for public savings is a kind of referendum in the belief that the State making the request, is and will remain solvent. The four bonds have been a success because 95% of the bonds were purchased by Major European multinationals, by European and American financial institutions, and also by European and American investors.

The success of the Ivorian bonds on international markets does take into account to primarily strengthen macroeconomic credibility, but Ivorian bonds are also attractive as an asset class, with yields averaging between 6 and 8% against 2-3% for Western markets.

Mrs. Kaba Niale, Minister in charge of Economy and Finance of Ouattara announced "The first challenge of our ministry in 2015 will be to mobilize significant resources on the money market and fund major projects for the emergence of our country. "And later Madame Minister stated that "All budgetary support from our partners in development was achieved. In total, 1.782 trillion has F.CFA been mobilized against 1.350 trillion FCFA.

The Minister Mahaman Gaya, former top economist at has ADB, and former minister of construction in Niger took part in an international conference in France, during that conference he presented a debt-based communication. For him, Cameroon. Cote d'Ivoire, Kenya, Niger debt represent 33 to 40% of their budget while social services account for only 10%.

According to Mr. Mahaman, today, all the experts agree that all of the debt of African countries is for them a bottleneck on the way of development.

So if the prospect of a promising growth encourages Ouattara and his donors optimism to emit bonds in dollars on the international market but it also raised worries about the sustainability indebtedness of the Ivory Coast.

Some observers believe that Cote d'ivoire still has a comfortable margin in order to take on more debt. Especially the Ivorian external debt represents 43% of gross national income in 2013, which corresponds to the average of developing countries. However, if this line exists, it is not so far a white card debt, for several reasons.

First, because debt levels should be assessed according to the repayment capacity - often limited for African economies. Even a debt representing 40 to 50% of GDP may be difficult to pay for a country like the Ivory Coast with structural political and economic fragility or a low budget revenues which between 20 and 40% of GDP.

Moreover, during the 1980s, countries that were subject to repeated defaults have been despite external debt ratio considered low for developed countries (less than 40% of GDP).

Second, in spite of a promising growth, insufficiently diversified Ivorian economy remains vulnerable to any economic shock: flipping over or a sharp fall in export earnings due to weak global demand. The dependence of the Ivorian growth in commodity prices, which are more volatile, is a vulnerability factor that could lead to rapid re-indebtedness.

Cote d 'Ivoire is therefore not immune to relapse and may encounter payment difficulties, and Ouattara must think especially to the eleven African countries that have reached the completion point of the HIPC initiative are low risk of debt distress. Furthermore, given the budgetary situation of the creditor countries, African countries could not count on a new episode of massive debt cancellation.

Third, if some emphasize the positive evolution of the Ivorian debt structure in the sense that domestic debt is becoming increasingly important, the fact remains that it is not free risk. Indeed, this internal debt, underwritten at much less favorable conditions, places a significant burden on public finances. Ivory Coast despite the attainment of the completion point of the HIPC initiative in 2012, faces pressure on funding because of the size of its domestic bank debt that must be refinanced regularly.

Fourth, remember that it is the public deficit, which feeds the debt. Unfortunately, since 2000 t Ivory Coast adopted expansionary fiscal policies (public investment, consumption subsidies) to cushion the effect of the crisis.

But what is ironic is that the high growth in the Ivory Coast has meant the development of very large fiscal deficits. Due to the discovery of natural resources, or the generous redistribution (wage increases, subsidies) for electoral purposes.

Finally, if Cote d'Ivoire has enjoyed over the last three years of investor appetite for yield thanks to ultra-accommodative monetary policies in the United States, Japan and Europe, the situation is now change. Indeed, investors are starting to demand higher interest rates to hold the debt of some African countries, a sign that the market has become more and more demanding and careful about rising budget deficits.

For example, Ghana was a few years ago an example for its middle class and its large reserves of oil, saw its borrowing costs rise. The issuance of $ 1 billion achieved last year with a rate of 7.88% is trading above 9% today. This may place African budgets under pressure and trap them in a debt spiral.

If we are still far from the catastrophic situation of the 80s, not taking into account the risks associated with poor debt management, including pursuing expansionary fiscal policies, politicizing public investment, making the electoral redistribution, lacked transparency in the management of public funds and maintaining the excessive weight of the State, is likely to undermine the hopeful dynamic economy and derail Cote d'Ivoire from the way of the emergence for many years to come.

CHAPTER 4

POVERTY, INEQUALITY AND UNEMPLOYMENT

The causes of the worsening poverty in Ivory Coast are to be found in the profound inequality that plagues our country. Cote d'Ivoire is a country with some of the largest reserves of strategic raw materials in the world.

Cheap energy sources, optimal opportunities for agricultural and livestock production, huge tourist attractions and a very good location in terms of economic geography

However, more than 80% of its 20 million are poor and more than two thirds of young Ivorian are unemployed.

First, it must be stressed that about 8% richest of the Ivorian population receive 60% of the national Ivorian income and the poorest 92% receive only 3% of this income.

In access to productive assets such as land. Considerable rural population does not access the most basic good of production. There are inequalities in education, because the richest 10% have a minimum of twelve years of schooling, while 70% with the lowest incomes barely reach five years of schooling. This results in lower wages, because the gap between the skilled and unskilled labor is one of the largest.

There are great inequalities in health, due to the lower life expectancy and maternal and infant mortality. Most of the diseases in 2010 and 2013 were associated with poverty which have caused the death of 2,600 children in Ivory Coast.

Poverty would have been half compared to that which currently exists if the Gbagbo' government program had been applied. The increase in inequality has doubled poverty. This is what I call "unnecessary" poverty, which caused only more inequality.

There are small and medium enterprises in the Ivory Coast, which are the main source of employment and that can generate more jobs, but they only receive 5% of the total volume of loans granted by the colonial banks in Cote d'Ivoire.

Ouattara's regime must address the eradication of poverty because the HIPC completion point is a major asset for poverty reduction. The clamor on inequality and poverty extends, because President Ouattara is not interested in the Ivorian daily life from all regions and all political parties.

Ouattara's government must be inspired by Brazil's Zero Hunger program, which is absolutely anti-inequality and develops an original strategy seeking to include the entire society to have access to food as a basic human right.

It should thoroughly discuss the problem of poverty and development. These are not magical keys, but any comparison between more or less unequal societies shows the importance of trust and confidence within a company's ability to associate, civic consciousness and ethical values.

From 2007 to 2010, remittances from Ivorian immigrants from Europe, North America, Africa, and the Middle East to help those who stayed in the Ivory Coast, accounted for 3 billion CFA. Resource flows did not enter into the calculations of traditional economists, and it is a kind of perfect capital, which does not generate foreign debt, but go to the areas that are most in social needs and have a multiplier effect important.

Ouattara should ultimately put the economy at the service of ethical values such as the right of families and children, or the young people to have a job and older people to be protected. 70% of people over sixty years in Cote d'ivoire have no resource. It must be an ethical responsibility in public policy and in the activities of private companies and political party that wants to lead the future of Ivory Coast should follow this model.

In 2012, the unemployment rate in Cote d'Ivoire was around 60%. The education system appears as if it has been specifically designed to increase the workers or work for existing industries and the public sector. Since the independence of some African countries most of these young nations began to train their citizens to take different positions because Africans had little or no education.

In Cote d'ivoire, education was geared toward taking a formal employment, but not to stimulate innovation. Employment was easily accessible if you could read or write. Sometimes the completion of education at the elementary or secondary level was sufficient to guarantee a job. Today, times have changed, but we have not changed with them. Even with a university degree, many jobs are lacking.

We spend 16 years or over to school to get a degree and then be unemployed. The remains of an archaic educational system have left us on the edges because too busy to feed a small capitalist class that has access to quality and cheap labor, to the detriment of the Ivorian youth.

Ivorian youth is the victim of an education system that make them to be employed or few who have access to capital. Students study Business Administration to administer the activities of others, but not to learn how to be entrepreneurs. Knowledge about the adhesion of different industries is not available. So that the population has increased, but employers remain low because innovation is low.

Investors help reduce poverty because they create jobs for African youth. They are however not the solution to unemployment. Investors essentially access to cheap labor. African youth can create jobs and invest in their own country. To reduce youth unemployment, but it must be equipped with entrepreneurial skills and know-how for entry into various industries and access to capital. This requires reform of the education system in Côte d'Ivoire.

To fight effectively against the problem of unemployment in the Ivory Coast and Africa as a whole, there must be an overhaul of the education system. For starters, we're used to an education that does not promote thinking, but encourages the consumption of knowledge.

There is nothing wrong with studying the knowledge available to us, but it's better to have an education system which encourages students to identify environmental problems and solve them by compiling knowledge that are available with new discoveries. An education system that is more theoretical than practical encourages students to cram information rather than thinking about how it can be applied to solve problems. Encouraging a practical approach training. Our students will be able to find problems around them and try to better resolve them

I salute the intellectual honesty of Mr Ousmane Diagana, Operation Director of the World Bank who stated to the international community, telling the truth about Cote d'Ivoire's economic situation. With a clear economic analysis that perhaps will help the Ivorian government to change their economic policy.

Ousmane has proven that he is neutral and that is not an activist of the RDR, much less a resonance chamber of RDR Ouattara political party as Mr. Madani Tall, former Director of Operations of the World Bank Côte d'Ivoire did during his mission in Cote d'ivoire.

It has been over 3 years since I published articles in online journals as Ivoirebusiness.net, Ivorian.net and economic magazines on poverty, inequality and unemployment in Ivory Coast, to bring my modest contribution to the Ouattara's government on economic issues, to improve the lives of my country mates although I am not member of its political party.

For example, between 2010 and 2013, the number of poor increased by 18 million, and their percentage is still increasing since Ouattara is in power.

First, it is important to mention that about 20% of the Ivorian population receive 60% of Ivorian national income and the poorest 80% receive only 3% of this income.

Access to productive assets, such as land is a serious issue. Population living in the rural area does have not access to the most basic good of production. There are inequalities in education because 10% of the richest have a minimum of twelve years of schooling while 70% have the lowest income barely reach five years of schooling.

This results in lower wages, because the gap between the skilled and unskilled labor is one of the greatest. There are great inequalities in health due to the low life expectancy and high rates of maternal and infant mortality. According to the World Bank From 2010 to 2013, diseases associated with poverty have caused the death of 2,600 children in Côte d'Ivoire. Poverty would have been half compared to that which currently exists if Gbagbo's program was implemented.

The increase in inequality has doubled poverty. This is what I call poverty "unnecessary poverty", which is caused solely by more inequality. There are small and medium enterprises in the Ivory Coast which are the main source of employment and that can generate a lot more, but receive only 5% of the total volume of loans granted by banks colonial Coast ivory

Ouattara must address the eradication of poverty because the HIPC completion point is a major asset for poverty reduction. The clamor on inequality and poverty spreads because Ouattara is not interested in the Ivorian daily life from all regions and all political parties.

The Ivorian population has welcomed the idea of the country's entry into the HIPC because they hoped to have excellent living conditions. According to the World Bank, that are close to 4, 60 billion euro debt than the Ivory Coast will not have to repay.

This is money that the government can use to rehabilitate Ivory Coast socially and economically. The 9% annual economic growth that

Ouattara has announced is not inclusive. Trade and external investment in commodity processing sectors represent less than 10 percent of GDP

An unemployment rate approaching near 60 percent, an inflation rate in double digits, runaway budget deficit, growing insecurity, democracy back, and 4 bonds in 3 years. The benefits of obtaining the HIPC completion point should improve the living conditions of the entire Ivorian population, and put all the Ivory Coast in Shipyard

Ouattara's government should implement a more inclusive development model for the well-being of the Ivorian population. The "inclusiveness" is not only the inclusion of results, but means designing policies to strengthen economic, social and territorial cohesion.

The objective of inclusive growth in our country has to ensure equal opportunities for all and benefit sharing. Financing adequate protection programs in the future, including the guarantee of fundamental rights of people living in poverty and enable them to live in dignity and to take an active part in society.

In addition, social spending and education are investments in terms of human capital essential for economic competitiveness to a real inclusion, growth and sustainable development. Despite the economic growth experienced by Côte d'Ivoire over the past two years and an optimistic outlook, two-thirds of the population lives below the poverty line.

The government of Ouattara must stop distracting us with extensive growth of 9%. The government must understand that inclusive growth is the new direction for the sustainable economic development.

The challenge is to manage the economic growth that provides opportunities from the Ivorian population with a particular focus on the poorest. The government of Ouattara should not only focus not on the extensive growth rates, but also on the type of growth that should advocate the creation of jobs, promoting access to finance for small and medium businesses, pay attention to the most needy, and make homeland security a priority.

The announcement of the growth rate in African countries do not reflect the standard of living of the African population, especially the lives of Ivorian. For 3 years we are witnessing a "bling bling economic" or the Ivorian government forecasts a growth rate of 10% in 2014.

I am not opposed to the notion of "extensive growth" but rather to get the government of Ouattara advocate for an "inclusive growth", which emphasizes that growth levels are not the ultimate goal, but redistribution of economic growth is also essential because the current indicators do not provide information about redistribution.

A poverty reduction program of Ouattara must follow the "Trickle down Theory" of Gbagbo which was to encourage the production and supply component of the economy by lowering the restrictions on the expansion of SMEs / SMIs, particularly corporate and investment. This was made by reducing marginal tax rates on income, by eliminating regulatory barriers and promote the flow of part of the wealth to the poorest of the population, although the Ivory Coast was divided.

Despite the economic growth experienced by Côte d'Ivoire over the past three years and an optimistic outlook, two-thirds of the population lives below the poverty line. The government of ouattara must stop distracting the all word with the concept of extensive growth of 9 to10%. The government must understand that inclusive growth is the new direction for the sustainable economic development.

Since April 11, 2011 Cote d'Ivoire is ruled by inconsistent economic decisions. We toured some villages and some cities and we have experienced the social and economic realities of the Ivorian population and some economic operators, but also listen to some and their proposals to improve their current situation.

Ouattara keep announcing that Cote d'ivoire will have a strong economic growth of 10% in 2014 and the effects will be felt by the population. He also stated that "The Ivory Coast will have a double-digit growth by the end of 2015 and aspires to become an emerging country has 2020".

According to Ouattara Ivorian people must wait until growth reaches 10% in order for them to benefit from this growth. Saying that Ouattara meant that Ivorian did not benefit yet from the economic growth.

Our researchers found widespread disrepair of the economic fabric but they also stated that Cote d'Ivoire has the potential and the means to rebuild this West African nation with all his sons and daughters without exclusion.

This recovery is expected from the interior. This also implies the consolidation of peace and security, sanitation of the institutional and regulatory environment, and the priority to be given to agriculture, livestock and fisheries, enlargement of tax base, rehabilitation of infrastructure, availability of electrical power, and support for private initiatives, and small and medium enterprises.

The consolidation of peace and security without which no sustainable economic activity cannot be deployed, and national reconciliation with the abandonment of the catch-up policy. The difficult living conditions, lack of discipline from FRCI and Dozo who are responsible of insecurity is not encouraging for the population and businesses.

Civil society and businesses in general, must operate according to the principles of law. The legal, judicial, administrative and Ivorian regulatory framework needs to operate the necessary adjustments to adapt to the changing international environment to attract investment and promote economic and social development.

The priority of agriculture, livestock and fisheries to cover the needs of the population whose deficit touch several products (maize, cassava, rice, yams, sugar, beans, fish, meat ... etc.) is more important.

Allow the supply of raw material industries and support and, with regard to the comparative advantage of each region, and the dynamics of recovery and development.

Physical infrastructure (roads, railways, bridges, ferries ... etc.) Must be rehabilitated to facilitate exchanges between rural and urban areas and enable farmers to access inputs and other necessary services that contribute to the increase agricultural production and procurement of manufactured goods. And also private companies that operate there, to improve the performance of their investments, including reducing the cost of economic activity.

Electrical Power shall be qualitatively and quantitatively increased to meet the needs of households and businesses. The energy deficit situation is even worse in rural and urban centers served in thermal energy due to outdated equipment. Furthermore, the electricity supplied is poor quality. It is characterized by sudden voltage drops, untimely cuts and load shedding. This causes significant harm to the normal operations of the companies.

The Head of State should encourage partnerships with foreign companies better structured, to benefit local business know-how, skills, and technology. As well as open to other markets that require highest demands. After more than 150 trips by Dr. Ouattara, I wonder how many business partnerships he has signed, especially as the unemployment rate of is around 60% and has not shown no sign of reduction and the Ivorian still eat one meal a day.

No sustainable economic development cannot be envisaged without the support of financing structures. The revival of the national economy necessarily involves improving the national financial system, which is the basic prerequisite to allow national banks to effectively fulfill their function, including encouraging savings and provide credit.

Despite the agricultural potential of Cote d'ivoire which growth is around 9%, Ivorian live in poverty and the government of Ouattara has not a coherent economic policy to eradicate poverty.

The way forward is through a deep transformation of rural areas to reorganize and transform traditional farms. The Head of State Ouattara must adopt the strategy of the seven pillars developed by UNIDO namely: increasing agricultural productivity; upgrading value chains, exploitation of local demand, regional, and international telephone building efforts and innovation capacity, promoting effective and innovative financing, encouraging the participation of the sector private, improving infrastructure and access to energy.

The government of Ouattara must take the 'Trickle Down Economy Theory' 'of President Gbagbo, that is to say, the runoff of wealth to the poorer population, allowing the rich remain rich to help the Ivorian population.

Media near Ouattara's media does not tell us the truth about unemployment in Cote d'Ivoire of Ivorian percentage of working age increases every day.

In June 2011, 25% percent of the population against 60% in 2012 was jobless and young Ivorian accounted for 85%. Ivorian youth of working age and who had a job represented 15% of all Ivorian of working age, so how can Ouattara's press claim that things have gotten much better since he came to power.

According to INS, official unemployment rate has increased to 60% percent in March 2012. So, how is it possible that President Ouattara has not the exact number of young people without jobs? During the election campaign he promised to create one million jobs in 5 years or 200 thousand jobs per year?

Of course, this is a total joke. But the truth is that the crisis of unemployment in Côte d'Ivoire has not been subsided. In fact, we are in a situation or things have become much worse while developed countries confront the problems of unemployment, in some countries this scourge has become a constant of the economic situation.

This is the case for example of Côte d'Ivoire where the unemployment rate is estimated at more than 60% although the authorities consider slightly below this bar. Can this unemployment be lowered? In the 1980s, it was not as high as today. He was for example 12 per cent in 1984. Things have deteriorated over time due to the wrong political choices of the authorities of this country.

I recently undertook a study on the application of the Okun's Law in Côte d'Ivoire. In less technical language: I tried to know if economic growth had an impact on the reduction of unemployment in Côte d'Ivoire.

Each increase of a percentage point in the unemployment rate corresponds to a slowdown of 0.325% in real GDP around trend variation. This means that the growth rate must grow faster than the rate of unemployment, and at very high rates for hope to significantly reduce the unemployment rate.

But it is not enough to have double-digit growth rates but it needed that this growth must rich in jobs. Ouattara must reform the structure of the economy including by multiplying the number of jobs. It is not easy to create jobs "to a shots of magic hand" but to release the employment potential of the Ivorian economy, Ouattara must eliminate its policy of "catching up" and reducing corruption, approaches and unnecessary and costly bureaucracy surrounding the creation of a company in Côte d'Ivoire. Unfortunately, the environment is not secured and barriers to enterprise creation are so high in Côte d'Ivoire.

Agriculture occupied an important place in the components of the Ivorian national production. Unemployment in this sector has never reached the Summit that we deplore today: agriculture occupied a large number of Ivorian. The mining sector, in the mere exercise of mining extraction, was never a real attic of jobs.

The mining sector has not created so many jobs. But the investment and entrepreneurship for agriculture, need a rural land reform and a clarification of property rights. Who would invest on land to which is attached a vague and an uncertain property right? Here again the incentives are catastrophic.

Huge lands of the country's natural resources must therefore be enlisted to finance this institutional infrastructure with clear property rights, but which comply with the customary rights (because it is not ethical to remove local people from their lands to sell it to strangers), incentives to develop the agricultural sector will finally be there.

Unemployment makes the life of the Ivorian population very difficult in a country where the purchasing power is already very low and relatively unstable. The scourge of unemployment should be the priority of Ouattara's government otherwise this population will continue to be one of the poorest in Africa.

The reduction of unemployment will be undoubtedly a difficult task, but is not a battle lost in advance when we ask the institutional conditions to entrepreneurship and the protection of property rights. The reform of formal institutions is a matter of political will and Ouattara must face it to enhance growth and reduce the unemployment rate

I am not opposed to the notion of "extensive growth" but rather to get the government of Ouattara to opt for an "inclusive growth", which emphasizes that growth levels are not the ultimate goal, but redistribution of economic growth is also essential because the current indicators do not provide information about redistribution. Despite the economic growth experienced by Côte d'Ivoire over the past three years and an optimistic outlook, two-thirds of the population lives below the poverty line.

CHAPTER 5

IVORIAN'S OPINION ON ECONOMY

In a survey conducted by economic intelligence bureau, we found that Ivorian are divided on economic issues and on party line. The following questions have been asked:. Question 1: Do you think the Ivorian economy has improved? .Question 2: Do you think that the Ivoirian economy worsened. 25% of Ivorian responded saying that the economy is improving. 59% of Ivorian think the economy is deteriorating, and 16% did not express their opinion.

At the level of political parties, 40% of Republicans (RDR) reported that the economy has deteriorated. 45% think that the economy has improved, and 15% did not express their opinion. As for the old party (PDCI). 59% have stated that the economy has deteriorated. 17% said it has improved and 24% has expressed no opinion. 80% of the FPI members have argued that the economy has deteriorated, 15% has expressed that the economy has improved, and 5% had no opinion.

Men and women had different opinions. Among men, 65% said that the economy deteriorated, and 30% mentioned that it has improved, and 5% had no opinion. 80% of the women stated that the economy has deteriorated, and 18% believe that the economy has improved, and 3% did not express their opinion.

There was a significant difference among farmers and people living in the rural areas. 85% stated that the economy has deteriorated since the first round of elections in Côte d'Ivoire against 15% who expressed that the economy is improving.

This telephone survey of 1,000 people was conducted in Ivory Coast and was conducted from March 1 to March 30, 2012 and has a margin of error of ± 3%. The survey results were weighted to be a representative sample of all Ivorian adults.

Unfair dismissal, unemployment, insecurity, financial scandals, unfair competition," catch-economic political, inflation, arbitrary arrests, and justice of the victorious are the reasons why the Ivorian have stated that Ouattara's economic policies and his famous government program (ADO SOLUTION) is a failure.

By the time Gbagbo took power, Cote d'Ivoire's economy had spent years being battered by sanctions but still remains the most highly-developed in WAEMU Africa.

In some senses, Gbagbo inherited an economy that was heading for bankruptcy. So, it was a difficult task to create a silk purse of an economy from the pig's ear left by president Bedie. However, many analysts pointed out "the infrastructure was neglected, and slowly inefficiency and corruption became serious problems.

When Gbagbo took power on the surface, at least, things looked good at the start. Inflation, which was running at 14% before 1994, fell to 5% within in 2003.' Cote d'ivoire budget deficit, which was 8% of the GDP in 1997, fell to 1.5% in 2004.

Madani Tall economist at the World Bank in Cote d'Ivoire pointed out that ivorian's economy has "essentially doubled in real terms" and growing at an average of 3.2% a year since 2002, as opposed to only 1.6% per annum for the 10 years prior to Bedie leadership.

He also pointed out that the real tax revenues have effectively doubled since 1995, which has enabled the government to expand social welfare.

Unemployment was a crucial issue and President Gbagbo was acutely aware of it. He declared that the situation is combined with falling education standards and a skills shortage. "We have developed a number of sectorial strategies especially focusing on skills development to meet these challenges," Said President Gbagbo.

Yet other analysts think the current pictures being painted of Cote d'Ivoire's economy are far too bleak. Yes, there are big problems they say, but that doesn't mean that Ivorian are incapable of finding big answers.

Economist Davie Roodt stated: "We still have time to fix certain negative trends, with strong political leadership we can turn the ship around, but strong leadership often lacks. We also have significant policy uncertainty because of weak leadership."

Gbagbo's economic legacy stems from the political freedoms for which he fought and won. It's a framework where, in theory at least, all Ivorian have the right to pursue their economic dreams.

As the busy lunchtime pedestrian traffic bustles around him in downtown Abidjan, Kouassi Kouame, who works at a computing firm, ponders the question of Gbagbo and his economic legacy. "He has done a lot [on economic freedom]," he says. "It's up to us to take it forward. It's up to us now."

Ouattara must understand that the future of a nation depends on its youth and its education system. So it is stunning how our famous university is closed because of a simple presidential election. Ouattara must prove that he can do better than Gbagbo and especially encourage foreign investors he was talking about in the last election to come tos2x invest in the Cote d'ivoire to create jobs for young people.

Increased unemployment is a potential risk of social instability. Ivorian continue to suffer and Cote d'ivoire is facing demographic challenges as its population of youth aged 15 to 24 years increase and access to jobs continues to be problematic.

The budget deficit and external debt, which is around 9 trillion of F.CFA threaten to make the Ivorian labor market even more difficult and exacerbate and a volatile situation for young people. Unemployment and underemployment of young people have social ramifications - because young unemployed are more likely to participate in conflict or illegal activities.

Gbagbo said in a speech "I want to take Cote d'Ivoire on the way to work and to a sustainable prosperity. On this path, we will build school that can ensure equal opportunities, implement a policy of health ensuring equal access to care, make available Ivorian to live in a decent environment." In view of the polls, Ouattara should play the card of appeasement by releasing all political prisoners and demand the return of President Gbagbo to initiate a real national reconciliation.

CHAPTER 6

FRANC CFA AND MONATARY SLAVERY IN AFRICA

The CFA Franc is the only colonial monetary system in the world to have survived to the colonization. The gradual introduction of this system is the result of strategic choices of France putting Colonization Company serving French economic interest.

The monetary scheme then set up by the administration of De Gaulle in 1945, was a singularity that remains unpublished to this day. The CFA was a -unit under the FF, with a fixed parity and convertibility, permanent, unlimited and reciprocal. Gold schema functioning has at the same time requires the existence of an account for each operation in the franc zone.

The CFA Franc is the common denomination of the municipality from 14 African countries member Franc Zone. It is the following states

- Benin, Burkina Faso, Ivory Coast, Mali, Guinea Bissau, Niger, Senegal, Togo (BCEAO)
- Cameroon, Gabon, Congo, Equatorial Guinea, Central African Republic and Chad which form the Economic and Monetary Community of, Central Africa (CEMAC), the Institute of issue is the Bank of Africa Centrals (BEAC)

The CFA franc was created December 26, 1945, day or France ratifies Bretton Wood and method has its first declaration of parity of the International Monetary Fund (IMF). He means "candid French Colonies"

Africa "and in 1958 he became" franc of the French Cooperation in Africa "().

Today, the name CFA franc means "franc of Financial Community of Africa" for all member countries of the UEMOA and CEMAC

The monetary policy governing such a diverse aggregation of countries is uncomplicated because it is, in fact, operated by the French Treasury only, without reference to the central fiscal authorities of any of the WAEMU or the CEMAC states.

Under the terms of the agreement which set up these banks and the CFA, the Central Bank of each African country is obliged to keep at least 65% of its foreign exchange reserves in an "operations account" held at the French Treasury, as well as another 20% to cover financial liabilities.

The CFA central banks also impose a cap on credit extended to each member country equivalent to 20% of that country's public revenue in the preceding year.

Even though the BEAC and the BCEAO have an overdraft facility with the French Treasury, the drawdowns on those overdraft facilities are subject to the consent of the French Treasury. The final say is that of the French Treasury which has invested the foreign reserves of the African countries in its own name on the Paris Bourse.

In short, more than 65% of the foreign reserves of these African countries are deposited in the "operations accounts" controlled by the French Treasury.

The two CFA Central banks (BCEAO and BCEAC) are African only in name, but have no monetary policies of their own.

The countries themselves do not know, nor are they told, how much of the pool of foreign reserves held by the French Treasury belongs to them as a group or individually.

The earnings of the investment of these funds in the French Treasury pool are supposed to be added to the pool but no accounting is given to either their central banks or the countries of the details of any such changes.

The limited group of high officials in the French Treasury who know the amounts in the "operations accounts", where these funds are invested and whether there is a profit on these investments are prohibited from disclosing any of this information the central banks of the African states.

This makes it impossible for African members to regulate their own monetary policies.

Three basic mechanisms have traditionally been used to control monetary growth in the CFA Franc Zone by the two central banks operating under the instructions of the French Treasury: In the central banks' operations accounts, interest is charged on overdrafts, and conversely, interest is paid on credit balances.

When the balance in a central bank's operations account falls below an agreed target level, it is required to restrict credit expansion, generally by increasing the cost to member countries of rediscounting paper with the central bank or by restricting member-countries' access to rediscounting facilities.

Credit provided by the central banks to the government sector of each of their member countries can be no larger than 20% of its fiscal revenue in the previous year.

However, this tight control by France of the cash and reserves of the francophone African states is only one aspect of the problem. The creation and maintenance of the French domination of the francophone African economies is the product of a long period of French colonialism and learned dependence by African states. For most of francophone Africa, central banks are given limited power.

These are economies whose vulnerability to an increasingly globalized economy is increasing daily. There can be no trade policy without reference to currency; there can be no investment without reference to reserves.

The politicians and parties elected to promote growth, reform, changes in trade and fiscal policies are made irrelevant except with the consent of the French Treasury which rations their funds.

President Abdoulaye Wade of Senegal has stated very clearly: "The African people's money stacked in France must be returned to Africa in order to benefit the economies of the BCEAO member states. One cannot have billions and billions placed on foreign stock markets and at the same time say that one is poor, and then go beg for money."

France use of the CFA Pact which is designed to prevent these former colonies from developing themselves with their own resources is as inhumane as any condition being inflicted by any other nation.

There are two separates CFA franc in circulation. The first is that of the West African Economic and Monetary Union (WAEMU), which has eight countries. The second is that of the Central African Economic and Monetary Community (CEMAC) which comprises six countries. This division corresponds to pre-colonial French West Africa (AOF) and French Equatorial Africa (AEF) with the exception of Guinea Bissau formerly a Portuguese colony and Equatorial Guinea formerly Spanish.

Each of this two monetary union issues its own CFA franc. The WAEMU franc is issued by the Central Bank of West Africa States (BCEAO) and the CEMAC CFA franc is issued by the Bank of Central African States (BEAC) since 1994, both currencies were pegged at 100 CFA to the French franc but, after France joined the Euro at a fixed rate of 6, 6597 French franc to one Euro.

The monetary policy governing such a diverse aggregation of countries in so complicated because it is, in fact, operated by French Treasury, without reference to the central fiscal authorities of any of the WAEMU and CEMAC states. Under the term of the agreement which set up these banks and the CFA, the Central Bank of each African countries is obliged to keep at least 65% of its foreign exchange reserves in an "OPERATION ACCOUNT" held at the French Treasury, as well as another 20% to cover financial liabilities.

Credit provided by the Central Bank to the government sector of each of their member countries cannot be no longer than 20% of its fiscal revenue in the previous year. However, this tight control by France of the cash and reserves of the francophone African states is only one aspect of the problem.

The creation and maintenance of the French domination of the francophone African economies is the product of a long period of French colonialism and learned dependence by African states. For most of francophone Africa, central banks are given limited power.

These economies whose vulnerability to an increasingly globalized economy is increasing daily. There cannot be no trade policy without reference to currency; there can noninvestment without reference to reserves. The politicians and parties elected to promote growth, reforms, changes in trade and fiscal policies are made irrelevant except to the consent of the French Treasury which rations their funds. There are many who object to the continuation of this system and Gbabgo is one of them that is why he deported to the ICC at The Hague.

In 2010, France has run of money, and has a massive public and bank debt. It has the largest exposure to both Greek and Italian debt and has embarked upon another austerity plan. Its credit rating is on the brink of losing its AAA status and the private banks are going to have a major haircut on its intra-European debts. Part of the reason it has been able to sustain itself so far is because it has had the cushion of the cash deposited with the French Treasury by the African states since 1958. Much of this held in both stocks in the name of the French Treasury and in bonds which have offset and collateralized a substantial amount of French gift.

GBAGBO AND OUATTARA FINANCIAL WAR

The two presidents want to control the BCEAO. Ouattara and Laurent Gbagbo battle for control of the Central Bank of West African States (BCEAO). A decree of Laurent Gbagbo ordered the requisition of the offices of BCEAO in Abidjan. A decision which Ouattara responded by announcing their closure.

The control of the Central Bank of West African States (BCEAO) is the scene of a bitter battle in Ivory Coast. Ouattara announced the closure of Ivorian branches of the West African Bank. It reacts to the decision of President Laurent Gbagbo recognized by the Constitutional Council on the same day, ordered by decree the requisition of the BCEAO offices after the bank had revoked its access to national accounts this weekend. These developments occurring after the forced resignation of the Ivorian BCEAO governor, Philippe-Henry Dacoury-Tabley, near Laurent Gbagbo and accused of having authorized the disbursement of some 60 billion CFA francs (€ 91.5 million) for his regime.

Unclear whether Alassane Ouattara has the ability to enforce the injunction. Forces loyal to outgoing president, heavily armed, were parked all day Wednesday front of the BCEAO offices. Information conformed by Jean-Baptiste Compaoré, acting president of the BCEAO. "On 26 January 2011, the premises of the Central Bank has been invested and the staff that was there was retained to perform various operations under the tasks assigned to the Central Bank," he said in a statement. "The BCEAO strongly protests against this requisition decision and the appointment of a National Director taken in flagrant violation of international commitments made by the State of Côte d'Ivoire," said the acting president. Faced with this situation, he decided that "for now, all the BCEAO agencies installed on the territory of Côte d'Ivoire are closed until further notice."(22)

The BCEAO is in the control and management of the Ivorian state. Besides the issue of banknotes in the eight member states of the West African Economic and Monetary Union of West, it is responsible for the centralization of foreign exchange reserves of the Union, the management of the monetary policy of its states members, bookkeeping Treasuries States of the Union and the definition of the banking law applicable to banks and financial institutions. Which was therefore a key element of the war engaged between Ouattara and Gbagbo?

Ouattara, elected by the international community decided to "immediately stop all exports of coffee and cocoa" in Côte d'Ivoire, the world's largest cocoa producer and exporter for a month.

This financial strangulation strategy practiced by Ouattara's purpose is to directly challenge the same ability of the incumbent to manage the Ivory Coast. A day later Gbagbo's regime decided the requisitioning of the BCEAO offices in Abidjan.

Ivorian President reacts to the waterfall closure of international banks in the country. After the Council of Minister President Laurent Gbagbo has decided to nationalize the Ivorian subsidiaries of French banks SGBCI, BICICI and BICICI, English Chatered Standard Bank, Citibank and American, because they did not respect the notice of giving three months before closure. In the official statement of his government, it is stipulated that the State, taking vis-à-vis its people and economic operators responsibility issued a decree that the State of Côte d'Ivoire take control by taking a full and complete participation in the capital of these banks.

The Director of SGBCI invoked security reasons to justify the temporary suspension of its activities. "We are facing one hand to the inability to operate almost normally trade-off between banks and the other, the short-term inability to ensure the supply of our boxes fiat currencies" had she said in a statement. Reasons which BICICI and Citibank few days later have added, the inability to ensure the safety of their employees.

Ivorian plunged into psychosis. Investors rushed to institutions to absorb liquidity. The queues at the ticket offices and entrance doors of the banks were at the alarming dimensions. At the beginning of the post-election crisis, the international community the international and ECOWAS

(Economic Community of West African States) in particular, favorable to Ouattara, have chosen strategy of economic suffocation to force the incumbent President Laurent Gbagbo to cede power to his rival.

On 26 January 2011, the Central Bank of West African States (BCEAO), common to the eight countries of the West African Economic and Monetary Union (UEMOA), ordered the closure of its management and national agencies in Côte d'Ivoire before announced their requisition. A closure that gradually paralyzed the Ivorian banking system.

Looking for a way to pay civil servants and the military, to finance its policy and reassure his fellow citizens, Laurent Gbagbo thought finding the parade by nationalizing subsidiaries of international banks that had ceased operations. The fundamental objective of the President of the Republic is to ensure the continuity of the opening of these banks in order to preserve jobs and to ensure access of citizens and economic operators of their assets provided that these assets are not the property of those banks, "said the statement issued after the Council of Ministers, which promises that every citizen and every trader will have access to his bank accounts as soon as possible.

The post-election crisis orchestrated by France requires Cote d'Ivoire stands out from France and gets rid of F.CFA to beat his own national currency. Today, the WAEMU member states have shown that they remain French oppression in Africa and UEMOA made no monetary integration object, against his mission was to facilitate the exchange, the free movement of goods and people, the commercial, industrial, agricultural, scientific and artistic between member states of the monetary union.

The final decision of the Council of Ministers and the Conference of WAEMU Heads of States and manipulations of French banks in Cote d'Ivoire; requires us to make firm decisions for the future of our country by creating our own Central Bank and beat our own currency to free blackmail of France to proclaim our economic independence.

According to the World Bank, the outstanding external debt of the Ivory Coast was at the end of 2009-6800 Billions of CFA franc for more than 48 years the external assets of the Ivory Coast were account for the operation of the French Treasury. So what is this famous operating account? And it is important that the Bank of France explains why Cote d'Ivoire should keep more than 65% of foreign assets in French Treasury, yet the Ivory Coast is an Independent State with 17 banks and three financial institutions.

The time has come for the Ivory Coast to take over its destiny. Ivorian are able to manage their foreign assets and to speculate on the New York Stock Exchange, London and Tokyo in the same way that France does with foreign assets of all Member States of the Franc Zone. The market economy is based on an organized banking system whose Ivory Coast needs. Developed countries have long implemented a quality banking system at the center of their concerns, their banking rate exceeds 80% by the Member States against the WAEMU are only a 10%.

During the 2010 election campaign, President Gbagbo said: "In Cote d'Ivoire, the financial sector still suffers from weaknesses or constraints to both institutional and structural that hinder its booming. And Community policy that we have chosen for money and credit limits opportunities for individual action by Member States. This means that the adjustment of bank resources to the specific needs of our economy and our people do not is our individual will" The Ivorian know that the French banks offer on-site services and little diversified product has a high cost. The people tired of all these manipulations of the French banks, says goodbye to the CFA, and welcome the new Ivorian currency.

Ivory Coast will have its Central Bank and three national banks (Agricultural Bank, Investment Bank, and Bank of Employment) that will assist economic operators and Ivorian businesses obtain consumer credit and funds to create businesses.

BIAO, SGBCI and SIB represent the interests of France. They always prefer to finance major French exporting companies of coffee and cocoa. These French banks have always provided funding to foreign economic operators that are in their game against the actual producers of wealth (farmers, ranchers, artisans, small and medium enterprises) are excluded from the banking system.

The creation of a new Central Bank is necessary. The Central Bank of Cote d'Ivoire (BCCI) will decide on the monetary policy of the Ivory Coast with the aim to stabilize prices, ensure full employment and facilitate economic growth.

- Oversee the entire banking system and publish reports to the Ivorian economy
- Act as lender of last resort
- Act on the external value of the new currency Ivorian through the use of policy rates (compensation of lenders) to motivate the coming and prevent capital flight. This therefore influence the money supply and economic growth of the new Ivory Coast. BCCI must be financially independent, receiving no government budget.

It will finance through interest on government bonds which it subscribed in the markets, the fees charged for the services to deposits and interest on the exchange of foreign currencies. BCCI be headed by a Governor and 5 Deputy Governors appointed by the President of the Republic and confirmed by the National Assembly of Cote d'Ivoire. Their mandate should be 5 years non-renewable. Despite this appointment process, the institution must remain independent of political power and the Governor is accountable to the Government and the National Assembly.

BCCI will have 5 Regional Central Banks located in the Bas-Sassandra, La Valle du Bandama, Moyen Comoé,18 Montagnes and Savane zone lead by five Vice Governors.

It is important for the BCCI to create a special department to print his national currency symbol of our sovereignty. This direction will also deal printable passport, national identity card, voter list, voter card also that secure documents such as tax stamp, auto thumbnails.

The convertibility of the new Ivorian currency will be easy. Businesses will be able to transfer so much capital, organize their repatriation without being limited by any amount or duration. The convertibility of the new Ivorian currency will be fixed according to the international banking norms.

The IMF defines the current convertibility, like all operations that do not affect the capital but allows to make payments (import-export, technical, commercial representation ... etc.) As for individuals they will not be outside of this practice.

They will receive an annual allowance per person which will be determined by the new Central Bank of the Ivory Coast to compensate for the expenses of such studies, care, tourisms ... etc. BCCI will have this of exchange because it is equal to our level of development.

The authorities will make an effort to make Cote d'Ivoire attractive. And also promote the emergence of a wealthy class which will support growth, and will fit into a market economy.

The New Central Bank must be vigilant as to the convertibility of the new currency in foreign currency, and it should not opt for the full liberalization of its short-term currency.

The exchange rate of the new currency will be determined in the interbank market. In this context, the local banks will exchange currencies freely at the negotiated rates; and the role of BCCI will be to regulate the liquidity in the market between supply and demand.

Cote d'Ivoire must stop to be manipulated by the Paris Club, London Club and the IMF that ruined many countries. Argentina was forced to privatize its entire economy by reducing the number workers and caused the collapse of its banking system.

Instead of waiting the macroeconomic indicators to turn green, Cote d'Ivoire and the Member States of the UEMOA should aim to beat their currencies in order to achieve economic independence.

Two crises in the field of international affairs and development, i.e., the worldwide great economic downturn and the Ivorian electoral stalemate, have raised a question about the relevance of the CFA Zone, a monetary union between francophone African countries and France and the European Union.

From colonization to present day, CFA zone countries are bound to an agreement with France to deposit the bulk of their foreign reserves in the "Operation Account" of the French Public Treasury.

This state of affairs undermines the monetary, financial, economic, and political sovereignty of francophone African countries with a fixed CFA to the Euro (until 1991 to the French franc).

The recession put in peril steady growth and development gains in sub-Saharan Africa. As the Euro survival quagmire continues to unfold, there are concerns about the CFA zone economies.

The electoral stalemate in the Ivory Coast gave France the opportunity to flex its political, military, diplomatic, and financial muscles. Financially, France has imposed economic sanctions against Gbagbo's regime by closing all French owned banks for month. Preventing ivorians to get access to their account.

This is one of the many examples of the precarious state of the economic independence of the Ivory Coast coupled with its un-sovereign nature.

The post-election crisis orchestrated by France require Cote d'ivoire to beat his own currency and get rid of CFA franc. Today WAEMU countries have shown that they remained French oppression instrument in Africa and UEMOA made no monetary integration object, which mission was to facilitate the exchange, the free movement of goods and people, the commercial, industrial, agricultural, scientific and artistic between member states of the monetary union.

The final decision of the Council of Ministers and the General Conference of WAEMU Heads of States and manipulations of French banks in Cote d'Ivoire; require Cote d'ivoire to take a firm decision by creating and beat its own currency in order to proclaim its economic independence.

According to the World Bank, the outstanding external debt of the Ivory Coast was at the end of 2009 over 8 billion dollars. For more than 50 years the external assets of the Ivory Coast were accounted in the operating account of French Treasury.

So what is this famous operating account? And it is important that the Bank of France explains why Cote d'Ivoire should keep more than 65% of foreign assets in French Treasury, yet the Ivory Coast is an Independent State with 17 banks and three financial institutions.

The time has come for Ivory Coast to take over its own destiny. Ivorian are able to manage their foreign assets and to speculate in the New York Stock Exchange, London and Tokyo in the same way that France does with foreign assets of all member states of the Franc Zone. The market economy is based on an organized banking system whose Cote d'ivoire needs. Developed countries have implemented a quality banking system at the center of their concerns, their banking rate exceeds 80% but the member states the WAEMU are only a 10%.

During the 2010 election campaign, Gbagbo said: "In Cote d'Ivoire, the financial sector still suffers from weaknesses or constraints to both institutional and structural that hinder its booming. And Community policy that we have chosen for money and credit limits opportunities for individual action for member States. This means that the adjustment of bank resources to the specific needs of our economy and our people do not fulfill our individual will. The Ivorian people know that the French banks offer on-site services and little diversified product with high cost. The people tired of all these manipulations done by French banks,

It is time to say goodbye to the CFA franc, and welcome the new Ivorian currency. Cote d'Ivoire will have its Central Bank and three national banks (Agricultural Bank, Investment Bank, and Bank of Employment) that will assist economic operators and Ivorian businesses obtain consumer credit and funds to create businesses.

BIAO, SGBCI and SIB represent French's interest. They always prefer to finance French major exporting companies of coffee and cocoa. These French banks have always provided funding to few economic operators that are in their game to deplete the Ivory Coast. And the actual producers of wealth (farmers, ranchers, artisans, small and medium enterprises) are excluded from the banking system.

The New Central Bank of Cote d'ivoire or (BCCI) will decide on the monetary policy of the country with the goal to stabilize prices, ensure full employment and facilitate economic growth. Oversee the entire banking system and publish reports to the Ivorian economy. Act as lender of last resort. Act on the external value of the new currency Ivorian through the use of policy rates (compensation of lenders) to motivate the coming and prevent capital flight. This therefore will influence the money supply and economic growth of Cote d'ivoire. BCCI will be financially independent.

And will be financed through interest on government bonds, and the fees charged on the deposits; and interest on the exchange rates.

BCCI will be headed by a Governor and Deputy Governors 5 appointed by the President of the Republic and confirmed by the National Assembly of Cote d'Ivoire. Their mandate should be 5 years non-renewable.

Despite this appointment process, the institution must remain independent of political power and the Governor is accountable to the Government and the National Assembly.

It is important for the BCCI to create a special department to print his National currency symbol of our sovereignty. This direction will also deal printable passport, national identity card, voter list, voter card also that secure documents such as tax stamp, auto thumbnails.

The Convertibility of CFA Franc to French Franc has maintained commercial and financial relations with its former colonies. This relationship is provided by parity and free convertibility of the French Franc to CFA franc.

Such a guarantee reassure French investors since no convertibility risk that will interfere with the regular repatriation of their profits. The convertibility benefis France and all French companies located in Franc zone.

The convertibility of the new Ivorian currency will be easy. Companies will be able to transfer so much capital, organize their repatriation without being limited by any amount or duration and the convertibility of the New Ivorian currency will remain current.

The IMF defines the current convertibility, like all operations that do not affect the capital but allows to make payments (import-export, technical, commercial representation ... etc.)

As for individuals they will not be outside of this practice. They will receive an annual allowance per person which will be determined by the new Central Bank of Cote d'ivoire to compensate for the expenses of such studies, care, tourisms ... etc. BCCI will have this system of exchange because it corresponds to our level of development.

The authorities should make efforts to make attractive Cote d'Ivoire and also promote the emergence of a wealthy class that will support growth and that will fit into the market economy.

The New Central Bank must be vigilant as to the convertibility of the new currency in foreign currency, and it should not opt for the full liberalization of its short-term currency.

The exchange rate of the new currency will be determined on the interbank market. In this context, the local banks will exchange currencies at freely negotiated rates; and the role of BCCI is to regulate the liquidity in the market to imbalance between supply and demand. .

Cote d'Ivoire must stop to be manipulated by the Paris Club, London Club and he IMF which has ruined some countries such as Argentina, which was forced to privatize its entire economy by reducing the number workers and had caused the collapse of its banking system.

Although today it seems utopian to some people, Cote d'Ivoire and the Member States of the UEMOA should aim to beat their currencies in order to achieve economic independence.

CHAPTER 7

NEW CURRENCY AND THE IVORIAN PUBLIC OPINION

The technique and methodology used to obtain the results of this poll is called 'Ivoirobarometres'. This technic is performed from telephone interviews ad 'hoc led to the request for a service or organization. Ivoirobarometres allow to focus on specific groups of probes when necessary.

According to Ivoirobarometres polls, Ivorians are favorable to the creation of the new Ivorians currency. 61% of Ivorians are in favor of the idea of creating a new currency and abandon the CFA franc and conversely 39% of surveyed Ivorians want to maintain the CFA franc and BCEAO. According to the survey, it also turns out that 70% of 30% of Ivorians who want to use the CFA franc as currency has a low level of education and only 30% have completed graduate studies

The survey was conducted among 1,000 people resident in Abidjan, Paris, London, and New York City on 15 December 2010 to 15 March 2011.

Before the elections, another survey found that 55% of Ivorians would like keep the CFA franc against 45% who opposed it because they considered that currency as an instrument of French rule in Cote d'Ivoire.

The idea of creating an independent state and proclaim its economic independence frightens many Ivorians. Unknowingly, Ivorians have experienced economic independence in the era of President Gbagbo.

Economic independence proclaimed by Gbagbo has allowed Cote d'ivoire to live for 10 years with a fixed budget and repay part of its external debt to the World Bank and the International Monetary Fund, the Paris Club and London Club.

THE NEW IVORIANS CURRENCY

France wishes that no member of the UEMOA and CEMAC countries be fully sovereign and Just as a sovereign country adopts a positive law, an army and various symbols of state (flag, national anthem and other symbols), and there, on the basis of its sovereignty is founded to beat its currency.

Most Ivorians civilizations (Kru, Mandee, and Akan) share traditional practices based on gold and silver. The choices of the name of the Ivorians currency may also be able to discuss national identity. The name of the Ivorians currency will be chosen between Dasika composed of Dasi (silver) well known in Kru and Mandee and Sika well known in Akan people to designate the gold, silver, and wealth. The advantage of this proposal is to enhance the cultural uses of a country in a monetary momentum.

International trade in goods and services or capital require the exchange of currency or currencies. The exchange system, set of rules that organize the exchange of currencies between them, is an important factor in the strategic choices.

Most countries of the world are subject to the floating exchange rate regime or flexible at the expense of fixed exchange rates became inoperative since the end of the Bretton Woods system in 1971 and officially disappeared in 1976 at the Kingston Conference in Jamaica.

The choice of Cote d'ivoire could be on the floating or flexible exchange rate regime. The advantage of such a scheme is theoretically provide the Central Bank of Côte d'Ivoire to intervene in the market to support the currency. The external balance is automatically performing the matching of supply and demand of foreign currency. In addition, the Treasury would be immune consecutive negative influences budget deficits of a reference nation under the fixed exchange rates.

FROM THE SOVEREIGN ROLE OF THE TREASURY

The treasury naturally represents the political authority that is to say the State. As such, it provides the guarantee of the entire financial and monetary system. This is the first money creation agent. It provides and manages the collection of taxes, runs the state expenditure, issues government securities and bonds. This is the real principal of the Central Bank of Côte d'Ivoire (BCCI). The choice of budgetary treasure influence the nation's economic life and affect the entire economic policy. All the monetary and financial system is built around the public treasury.

MACROECONOMIC REFORMS

The Ivorians economy needs to be rethought in the light of the concept of political sovereignty economy. An economy capable of propelling its own dynamic. The goal is to make Côte d'Ivoire a relatively strong emerging economy in the space of a decade, in the sub-region and in the world, why not?

- The main operation should be primarily focused on its internal resources, the outside being only a supplement;
- The decisions taken, the activities and the production system itself should give priority to the internal needs of Côte d'Ivoire.

Macroeconomic reforms must involve one hand, major economic aggregates and secondly, the restructuring of economic sectors.

The main aggregates:

All government interventions must contribute to the achievement of the famous magic square; that is to say ensuring:

- GDP growth;
- Growth of employment, thus reducing unemployment;
- Price stability, so the fight against inflation;
- And finally, the external balance by surpluses in the trade balance.

Possible ways and achieve target (magic square) are the following:

- Monetary policy, acting on interest rates;
- Tax Policy (increase or decrease, Structural reforms

The crucial point to prevent that Cote d'ivoire is controlled by France is the issuance of a national currency. No country could claim to be sovereign if it does not issue its own currency, interest-free and debt-free.

Today, the UEMOA and CEMAC member countries prefer to borrow from French Private banks money that they create without interest, which is an act of high treason, because he who controls the issuance of the currency of a nation ends up controlling all the policies of this nation. Meyer Amschel Rothschild, the founder of the largest banking dynasty in Europe: "Let me issue the currency of a nation, and I plug me who makes its laws."

We would like to make believe to Canadians that it would be a good thing for Canada to abandon the Canadian dollar for US currency – just as the countries of the European Community gave up their national currencies for the Euro - but this would be the end of the sovereignty of the Canada.

There is therefore no question of issuing money no matter how, without limits, and creating galloping inflation, as the opponents of any monetary reform like to repeat to scare African economies.

THE MISLEADING ROLE OF BCEAO

Today the BCEAO manipulated by the French Treasury usurped the sovereign power to create money (the BCEAO creating less than 5% of all the money of the nation), and seek to consolidate his power.

Paying not paper money, but 'scriptural' money (checks, or figures exist even on paper, but only in smart cards and computers, in the form of electronic signal), banks charge high interest on this money that they create in a single drop of ink (or a single key on a computer keyboard), then the value of money is based on the production of the country which belongs not to the BCEAO, but to the entire population of the country as a whole all Ivorians citizens should know that it is quite ridiculous, senseless and criminal for a country to borrow money that they can create themselves.

Yet once again, we are not talking to issue money no matter how, but according to the amount of existing products and our GDP then, Côte d'Ivoire could finance without interest all the needs of the nation, and pay our debts.

If any natural disaster occurred the financial assistance for the population and for reconstruction will come from the Central Bank of Cote d'ivoire. The government could supplement using its own Central Bank to create money without interest, while with this Treaty the UEMOA, it is forbidden for any Government to decide to give assistance.

Today the objective of the BCEAO is not at all to issue money according to the needs of the population, but to make more profits, and bring Governments, companies and individuals to go into even more debt.

France knows very well that if Cote d'ivoire start to control of the issuance of its currency, it would be a mortal blow to their monopoly of the credit creation, Côte d'Ivoire would give the example that a country can function without borrow from private banks, and all other countries will take the steps. This is why, by installing a single Central Bank France make it impossible for UEMOA member countries, to create its own currency whatsoever.

Why close hospitals, reduce public services or privatize, while the physical possibilities of providing these services - materials and labor - exist? With an honest money system, it would be possible to fund interest-free and debt-free what is physically feasible, to meet the needs of the population.

The Director General of the International Monetary Fund visited the headquarters of the Central Bank of West African States (BCEAO). Received by the Governor Tiémoko Meyliet Koné, the two personalities have maintained the economic situation of the 8 members of the integrated economic area.

After his working session with the authorities of the BCEAO, Christine Lagarde introduced a paper entitled "Financial integration in the service of inclusive growth." Before an audience of personalities, financial structures managers, researchers, students and actors of economic life, the International Monetary Fund Managing Director called for stronger economic growth and better shared in the economic area money west Africa.

According to Christine Lagarde, financial inclusion is to avoid failure of innovative projects for lack of funding. And according to her, only further financial inclusion helps reverse this trend. On this basis, the Director General of the International Monetary Fund sets out four requirements which, while not sufficient, is essential to achieve financial inclusion. For her, it is necessary to "strengthen the regulatory framework (...) maintaining stability, ensuring healthy development of micro-finance institutions, promote the development of innovative financial instruments."

In his contribution to the questions raised and insights gained by the Director General of the IMF, the Governor Tiémoko Meyliet Koné recalled the unceasing efforts of the BCEAO for banking supervision in the UEMOA zone. According to the Governor, despite the tensions that rocked some countries (Ivory Coast, Mali) with various crises, UEMOA is undergoing a period of "productive stability." And for him, the economic and monetary space is part of the West African regions of Africa where microfinance is the most developed.

"The BCEAO place an ambitious agenda," recalls its Governor. For Mr. Kone, this translates it free fees on certain banking services determined by the institution there are few months. This policy ensures he will continue with "reducing costs of financial offers" and "promotion of mobile financial services." Tiémoko Meyliet koné also held recalled the "constraints management on savings." Therefore, Lagarde assured him of support of the International Monetary Fund in all efforts BCEAO is going in the direction of greater financial inclusion and a more integrated economic zone.

Economic inclusion is a term used to describe a variety of public and private efforts aimed a bringing underserved consumers into the financial mainstream. UEMOA should use partnerships and initiatives focuses not only on expanding the availability of safe. Affordable products and services, but also on educating consumers about ways to become fully integrated into the banking system of the entire so called monetary union.

CHAPTER 8

COLONIAL BANKS AND TERRORISM BANKING IN COTE D'IVOIRE

The creation of a national currency is the key to the development of an economy; by creating money to lend to individuals and businesses, the central bank and / or the state creates economic development through consumption and investment.

The member states of the UEMOA and the CEMAC cannot be independent because they are caught in the terrorism of franc CFA and the French treasury.

The BCEAO is a branch of the Bank of France and the government the power to control the execution of the budget; development plans, existing financial arrangements, to the point for assessing the advisability of investing in a company.

The French Treasury operates in the member states of the UEMOA through the colonial banks. In Cote d'Ivoire, BIAO, SGBCI, BICICI and SIB are considered colonial banks and fully play the role of the Bank of France. These banks are managed with external management methods and French risk analysis.

These banks love to lend to Ivorian workers (payday loan, funeral loan, and school loan ... etc.) who consume imported products from France. In general, these banks refuse to lend to farmers and operators under the pretext that they do not offer guarantees.

The seasonal credit by which these colonial banks lend money some traders to buy and market the coffee and cocoa is the preferred method of funding for these banks. They refuse to finance the production because they believe the planters of coffee and cocoa will become rich and difficult to control.

The financial market does not fully play its role because of the lack of Local savings. The companies listed in the stock exchange of Abidjan struggle to reach Ivorian businesses. It is not because of the weakness of local savings but because of the refusal of French companies to cede part of their share to Ivorian investors. French companies may open branches in Cote d'Ivoire which will have, credit from those colonial banks who operate under the control of the Bank of France, which can easily refinanced through the BCEAO and the Bank of France.

The nationalization of these banks represent a long-term shot in the arm for the Ivorian economy. These colonial banks were not created to promote productivity but exploit Cote d'Ivoire raw material reserves and sell their manufactured products.

The idea of nationalizing a bank scare many people but some well-known economist such as Raymond J. believes that the nationalization of banks is essential: it restored a form of transparency and, at the same time, citizens' confidence in the banking system.

The same goes for the Nobel Prize in economics Paul Krugman, who made a statement on his blog saying that "The involvement of the US government in banks is the only solution to the current crisis". An analysis that Greg Mankiw formally contradicted on his blog: for him the fears about nationalization of banks are justified. "Why people are afraid of the idea of nationalization? The first reason is that it shows how the situation is serious.

The second reason, more solid it is that this advanced solution in the wrong direction. I absolutely do not want to be the government that decides who deserves credit or not, and what are the investments that deserves to be financed or not. This is a step towards crony capitalism; or those with political ties are in pool position." The analysis of the illustrious economist

Greg Mankiw points us in a discussion of cronyism, corruption, and poor stewardship of public funds. For us who know President Laurent Gbagbo, we are confident that the president elected by the people of Cote d›Ivoire always advocated good governance and fight against favoritism, nepotism and tribalism.

Crony capitalism that Greg Mankiw is talking about will not be tolerated in the new Ivorian banking system. President Laurent Gbagbo had no alternative choices but to nationalize these colonial banks. If he did not nationalize these colonial banks, the banking system would collapse like a house of cards, and the Ivory Coast would be in a similar situation to that which followed the crisis of the 30s in America: A deep recession, the multiplication of Ivorian business failures, the explosion in unemployment, falling of minimum wages.

These colonial banks in Ivory Coast had not experienced Lehmann type of bankruptcy in the United States. These financial institutions called colonial banks received instructions from their headquarters located in France that is why during the post-election crises they have closed most of the banks operating in Cote d'ivoire. The closure of these banks is considered an act of terrorism against the Ivorian because they did not inform the government and their customers of their decision.

Each Ivorian must understand that it is time to change the way things have been done in the past. Nationalizing banks will solve their problems if we do not change ourselves. Ivorian must choose banks that are about to perform a work ethic. Because it is exactly Ivorian hope to see in nationalization. Behavior of Justice Hope and fair treatment must the key point of any financial operation.

CHAPTER 9

FUTURE POST- ELECTORAL
CRISIS TO PREVENT

It is generally accepted that democracy is a form of government in which the people exercise sovereignty. Abraham Lincoln, stated that democracy is "government of the people by the people and for the people." In this sense, democracy is opposed to any power that is not the emanation of people.

In a true democracy, the holder of power is the people called primary sovereign. Citizens cannot exercise any sovereignty; they delegate their power to a number elected officials who exercise for them. They are designated through free and transparent elections.

Unfortunately, many countries in Africa have a facade of democracy, caricatured. One is certainly talking the polls but the result is not expression of the sovereign will of the people but rather the power of the prince. As a result, leaders become, over time, less and less inclined to accept the control of the people. Democracy then becomes the power of the stronger, the stronger and stronger.

Now to the 2015 elections themselves which are not only central to this dialogue, but also significant in making Africa the winner. Of course elections are very important in democracy, especially in emerging democracies, like ours.

It was the former UN Secretary-General, Kofi Anan, who said that "when citizens go to the polls and cast their votes, they aspire not only to elect their leaders, but to choose a direction for their nation" and according to him, only elections with integrity can bolster democracy, while flawed elections undermine it.

I agree with Kofi Anan's assertion, but how do we ensure that the 2015 elections in some countries in Africa would turn out to be of integrity in order to avoid undermining our nascent democracy? How do we conduct elections with integrity using the so-called "stomach infrastructure" by attracting votes with 5kg bags of rice?

How do we ensure elections with integrity in a situation in which almost all the outgoing Presidents, regardless of party affiliation, anoint their chosen successors prior to elections, thereby disregarding people's choices? And those who still have the opportunity to seek re-election for another term are given automatic ticket, regardless of their performance, thereby not only blocking other contenders from exercising their rights to participate, but also denying people the right to choose their leaders?

Elections are often synonymous with "disorders" and with no less than six major elections scheduled for 2015, the uncertain future of haunting is already beginning to settle in some West African countries.

Presidential elections are scheduled including Burkina Faso, Côte d'Ivoire, Niger, Nigeria, Guinea and Togo. In Burkina Faso and Nigeria especially, the tension is palpable and has already attracted strong misgivings about the possible outbreak of unrest.

President Blaise Compaore in power since 1987 wanted to hold a referendum to amend Article 37 of the Constitution relating to the limitation of the presidential mandate is the basis of a great discontent among the opposition and civil society. And he lost power by a popular revolution.

Democratic Republic of Congo has so far escaped serious upheaval due to its internal stability and a strong security apparatus. But the deteriorating political climate in 2015 could make the country more vulnerable,

The amendment of the Basic Law, including articles limiting the presidential term is the new discovery of "potentates" on the continent, but recent history has shown us that it was fatal for Mamadou Tandja of Niger.

A similar situation will occur in Togo where President Faure Gnassingbé wants to seek a third term when his opponents are calling in vain for constitutional and electoral reforms. These reforms interests include limitation of the presidential term, and the adoption of a voting system in two rounds.

In Nigeria, President Goodluck Jonathan, already greatly weakened by the wave of deadly violence that Boko Haram insurgents have settled in the country since 2009, under strong protest within his own party, the People's Democratic Party (PDP).

President Jonathan who finished the mandate of Umaru Yara'adua, who died in 2009 was elected two years later. In February 2015, he will be running for re-election under the banner of the PDP. No doubt the next developments in the security level will impact the election in a country where the Boko Haram sect has come to prove that it can strike at anytime and anywhere.

Ivorian and Guineans are still recovering from the pain of their previous presidential elections, and try to initiate a difficult standardization coupled with the economic recovery. Yet nothing says that the old demons will not resurface and plunge both countries with great potential in chaos

West Africa is at the edge of a critical period. These elections will take place in highly polarized societies and amid deep political divisions. A political common front is needed to fight against security threats in the context of the next presidential elections in West Africa.

CHAPTER 10

N0 CHANGE FOR WESTERN POLICY IN AFRICA

France has left a legacy of a colonial education system in most of the francophone countries. Fifty years after independence, what remains to Africa? Did the colonial education system helped Africans to be independents. And ready to freely elect their leaders.

Europe still has a control on African economies. And still keep manipulating elections in Africa in other to install their puppets ready to export the raw materials to the European markets.

The colonial education was the instrument used to brutalize Africans and inculcate the lower human mentality. And to make Africans believe that the white man is superior.

The colonial education did not help African countries industrialize their economy. But rather to steal the resources of African countries. Emergence of new social and political structures and even the education model was decided by external settlers.

Many questions remain asked. How to explain the failed democracy in Africa. The elections whose winners are chosen by outsider who are ready to finance rebellions. And chase leaders with nationalist and Pan-African vision.

The education in Africa has a Community character. The village participates on the education of the child even if a particular place went to parents, or people of the family clan. This education takes into account the wealth of the rural environment and It is usually through speech.

This African education is active and democratic. First, because, it flows into the action, participation, partitioning between theory and politics. And acquired empiric Knowledge, and a deep experience of value which is highly personalized.

The concept of group cohesion is important - each group member must play its part, and respect the rules and community values. The personal development is valued but the safety, perfection of the group. And democratic plurality is the cornerstone of the all process.

The settlers prefer African leaders who are not unanimously accepted among their people and who does not have the legitimacy among African people. And always ready to defend westerners interests.

In Francophone Africa, only minority elite serving the colonial administration did receive most of the economic benefit. And the best job opportunities available in the entire region

Gbagbo, a pan-Africanist advocate to reform education in Africa. He has always hoped that African schools serve African people and take into account the economic and political realities of the African continent.

At the inauguration of President Gbagbo, December 4, 2000 at the presidential palace. He said "the sovereignty of the Ivory Coast which I am responsible is not negotiable. And we don't rely on anyone to become king. One that makes you king still has a right to your seat".

Gbagbo message is filled with hope in education, economic, and political independence. And represent the proclamation of a new era based on the win-win partnership. And the end of the French colonial education system in Ivory Coast.

It is a duty for every African to seek to understand the issue of the eviction of President Laurent Gbagbo. Every crisis has its good side. One who has not been educated by this crisis will never understand the struggle of African leaders. It is also a duty for us to think of this crisis in order to draw lessons for the future.

Gbagbo is synonymous with the end of colonial education in cote d, ivory and francophone Africa in particular. This eminent politician who continues to fight for the total independence of his country, and for the dignity of the black man.

Encourage me to support others who will imitate his vision of a new Africa for Africans. I have always been convinced that President Gbagbo remains an example of a politician and a model that deserves to be taught in universities.

NOTES

1. Zounmenou, David (2011). "Cote d'ivoire post electoral conflict: What is at?". African Security: 48-55
2. "World Leaders back Ouattara as Ivory Coast Poll Winner",. BBC News, 3 December 2010
3. Roy, Debarati (2010). Sugar jumps to highest since February, coffee gains drops". Bloomberg. Archived from the original on 1 November 2010. Retrieved 4 December 2010
4. Ivory Coast's Gbagbo defies world leaders. www.euronews.com
5. Idem
6. US Economy (2014). Trickle Down Economics and Its Effects. Useconomy.about.com. Article Updated, August 27, 2014
7. Muhammad. Yunus (2007)> Creating a World with Poverty: Social Business and The Future of Capitalism, 31-34
8. Idem 41
9. www.ivoirebusiness.net; gbadosahoua.blogspot.com; africaview. net; gbabgo-ci.net; ladepechedabidjan.info. Les Performances Economiques de Gbagbo. October 2, 2011
10. Idem
11. Idem
12. Idem
13. Idem
14. Idem
15. Idem
16. Idem
17. Idem
18. Idem
19. Idem
20. Idem

SELECTED BIBLIOGRAPHY

Expert de l'ONU pris pour cible- Coted'ivoire –Politique –Actualites Internationales- FRANCE 2: toutes les informations internationales en direct= France 2". Info.france 2. Retrieved 23 April 2011.

Nossiter, Adam (4 April 2011). "Strikes by U.N. and France Corner Leader of Ivory Coast". *The New York Times*.

Une Suédoise de l'Onuci tuée par balle à Abidjan, *Le Point*

. Appablog.wordpress.com. 1 April 2011. Retrieved23 April 201 "Côte d'Ivoire. Vendredi: un "chaos généralisé" selon l'Onu - Conflits" (in French). Ouest-france.fr. Retrieved 23 April 2011.

"Côte d'Ivoire - Des jeunes incendient un véhicule civil de l'Onuci et font un blessé". Afreekelection.com. Retrieved 13 March 2011.

"Trois Casques bleus blessés dans une embuscade à Abidjan". *Le Point*. France. 14 January 2011. Retrieved 18 February 2011.

Par Europe1.fr avec AFP (29 December 2010). "Côte d'Ivoire : un Casque bleu blessé". Europe1. Archived from the original on 28 January 2011. Retrieved 18 February 2011.

"Abidjan: 3 Casques bleus blessés par les forces pro-Gbagbo, accuse l'Onuci". Google. AFP. Retrieved 6 March 2011.

"BBC News - Q&A: Ivory Coast crisis". Bbc.co.uk. 13 April 2011. Archived from the original on 22 April 2011. Retrieved 23 April 2011.

"UN troops surround Gbagbo's last defenders | Top News | Reuters". Af.reuters.com. 7 April 2011. Retrieved 23 April 2011. New proof of Ivory Coast vote killings *AP*

Ivory Coast: Ouattara fighters 'capture Yamoussoukro, BBC News - "UN: Ivory Coast Crisis Not Over Yet". VOA news. 11 April 2011.

David Lewis and Loucoumane Coulibaly, "Ivory Coast's Ouattara wins vote - election chief", Reuters, 2 December 2010.

David Lewis and Tim Cocks, "Ivory Coast seals borders after opposition win", Reuters, 2 December 2010.

Christophe Koffi, "Ouattara named winner of I. Coast election", AFP, 2 December 2010.

http://abidjan.usembassy.gov/ivoirian_constitution2.html

"Ivory Coast poll overturned: Gbagbo declared winner". BBC news. 3 December 2010.

"Constitutional body names Gbagbo I. Coast election winner", AFP, 3 December 2010.

"World leaders back Ouattara as Ivory Coast poll winner", BBC News, 3 December 2010.

Tim Cocks and Loucoumane Coulibaly, Ivory Coast's Gbagbo sworn in despite poll row, Reuters, 4 December 2010.

Tim Cocks and Loucoumane Coulibaly, "Ivory Coast's Gbagbo sworn in despite poll row", Reuters, 4 December 2010.

Roland Lloyd Parry, "Defiant Gbagbo sworn in as I. Coast president", AFP, 3 December 2010

"Thabo Mbeki to mediate in Ivory Coast president crisis". BBC News. 5 December 2010. Archived from the original on 5 December 2010. Retrieved 5 December 2010.

"'God has given us victory', Gbagbo's wife tells rally". France24. Retrieved 6 March 2011

"Ivory Coast women defiant after being targeted by Gbagbo's guns" (article). *The Guardian* (London). 11 March 2011. Retrieved 11 March 2011

Smith, David (1 April 2011). "Ivory Coast's well-armed rebels making quick work of revolution" (article). *The Guardian* (London). Archived from the original on 13 April 2011. Retrieved 1 April 2011.

Voice of America. 18 December 2010. Retrieved 8 January 2010.

"Special session of Human Rights Council on Côte d'Ivoire concludes after adopting a resolution calling for end to all human rights violations". United Nations Human Rights Council. 23 December 2010. Retrieved 8 January 2011.

"Ivory Coast: 'Disappointment' at UN's response to worsening situation". Amnesty International. 24 December 2010. Retrieved 8 January 2011.

Despite Growing Pressure, Ivory Coast Incumbent Gbagbo Still Has Outside Allies*VOA*

Ivory Coast's Gbagbo defies world leaders, euronews.com, 4 Dec 2010

Olivier Monnier and Pauline Bax. "Mbeki in Ivory Coast to Mediate as Gbagbo, Ouattara Each Claim Presidency." Bloomberg, 5 December 2010.

AU mediator Thabo Mbeki leaves Ivory Coast without a breakthrough, BBC World Service, 7 December 2010.

Gualbert, Phal (27 January 2011). "Gabon police tear gas protesters, tensions rise". Reuters. Archived from the original on 7 February 2011. Retrieved 18 March 2011.

Eric Agnero (28 December 2010). "African leaders arrive in Ivory Coast to deal with political crisis". CNN. Retrieved 28 December 2010

Indira A.R. Lakshmanan and Flavia Krause-Jackson, «U.S. Urges More Peacekeeping Troops, Sanctions to Stem Ivory Coast Chaos," Bloomberg, 22 December 2011. *BusinessWeek*. 16 December 2010. Archived from the original on 30 December 2010. Retrieved 31 December 2010.

"At least 20 killed in Ivory Coast clashes". *Boston Globe*. 16 December 2010. Retrieved 18 February 2011.

Aboa, Ange (10 January 2011). "Clashes in west Ivory Coast have killed 33: medic". Reuters. Retrieved 18 February 2011.

Aka, Evelyne (13 January 2011). "Ivory Coast curfew after 11 killed in Abidjan". Herald Sun. Retrieved 18 February 2011.

"Deadly clashes in Cote d'Ivoire - Africa". Al Jazeera English. Archived from the original on 14 March 2011. Retrieved 13 March 2011.

Smith, David (21 December 2010). "Death squads attacking Ivory Coast opposition, claims spokesman". *The Guardian* (UK). Retrieved 23 December 2010.

"Ivory Coast crisis: 'Nearly 450,000 refugees'". BBC News Online. 11 March 2011. Archived from the original on 12 February 2011. Retrieved 12 March 2011.

Andrew Harding (3 April 2011). "BBC News - Ivory Coast: UN presses Ouattara over Duekoue massacre". Bbc.co.uk. Archived from the original on 8 April 2011. Retrieved23 April 2011.

[b] "BBC News - Ivory Coast: Power and water cut to pro-Ouattara north". BBC News. 2 March 2011. Archived from the original on 5 March 2011. Retrieved 6 March 2011.

Drew Hinshaw (31 March 2011). "In Ivory Coast, Gbagbo's forces defect en masse: reports". Dakar, Senegal.

AP / RUKMINI CALLIMACHI Sunday, 12 December 2010 (12 December 2010). "Alassane Ouattara Governs Ivory Coast from Hotel". *TIME*. Retrieved 23 December2010.

"BCEAO : le gouverneur Dacoury-Tabley démissionne / Le gvt Gbagbo "rejette" la démission du chef de la banque ouest-africaine". Ladepechedabidjan.net. Retrieved18 February 2011.

"BBC News - Ivory Coast: Laurent Gbagbo orders bank branch seizures". BBC News. 26 January 2011. Archived from the original on 15 February 2011. Retrieved 18 February2011.

"Ivory Coast Crisis Hurting Economy, Ouattara Says". *Businessweek*. 19 January 2011. Retrieved 18 February 2011.

"Cote d'Ivoire's declining economy - Africa". Al Jazeera English. 17 October 2010.Archived from the original on 1 December 2010. Retrieved 4 December 2010.

Roy, Debarati (29 October 2010). "Sugar Jumps to Highest Since February; Coffee Gains; Cocoa Drops". Bloomberg. Archived from the original on 1 November 2010. Retrieved 4 December 201

"West Africa Exchange Closes Indefinitely After Gbagbo Seizure". *Businessweek*. 8 December 2009. Retrieved 18 February 2011.

"West African bourse reopens, was shut by troops: staff | Reuters". Af.reuters.com. 11 February 2011. Retrieved 18 February 2011.

"Ivory Coast Violence Drives Regional Stock Exchange to Mali". *Businessweek*. 25 February 2011. Archived from the original on 16 April 2011. Retrieved 6 March 2011.

"BBC News - Ivory Coast rush to withdraw bank cash". BBC News. 16 February 2011.Archived from the original on 17 February 2011. Retrieved 6 March 2011.

"Ivory Coast's Gbagbo seizes 4 international banks". *BusinessWeek*. 18 February 2011. Retrieved 6 March 2011.

"BBC News - Ivory Coast rush to withdraw bank cash". BBC News. 17 November 2010.Archived from the original on 17 February 2011. Retrieved 18 February 2011.

"How Ivory Coast's Gbabgo aims to solve his cash woes". CSMonitor. com. 23 February 2011. Archived from the original on 27 February 2011. Retrieved 6 March 2011.

Jah, Abu Bakarr (2010). "Democracy and civil war: Citizenship and peacemaking in Côte d'Ivoire". African Affairs 109 (437)

Collier, Paul (2010). «Meltdown in Côte d›Ivoire». *Wars, Guns, and Votes: Democracy in Dangerous Places*. New York: Harper Perennial. pp. 155–168.

Zounmenou, David (2011). "Côte d'Ivoire's post-electoral conflict: what is at stake?" African Security Review (1): 48–55.

Thousands Flee Ivory Coast as President Gbagbo Refuses to Cede Power - video report by Democracy Now!

Abadie, Alberto. 2005. "Semiparametric Difference-in-Differences Estimators", Review of Economic Studies, 72: pp. 1-19.

Alesina, Alberto and Robert J. Barro. 2002. "Currency Unions", Quarterly Journal of Economics, 117: pp. 409-436.

Anderson, James E. 1979. "A Theoretical Foundation for the Gravity Equation", American Economic Review, 69: pp. 106-116.

Anyanwu, John C. 2003. "Estimating the Macroeconomic Effects of Monetary Unions: The Case of Trade and Output", African Development Review, 15: pp. 126-145.

Arellano, Manuel and Stephen Bond. 1991. "Some Tests of Specification for Panel Data: Monte Carlo Evidence and an Application to Employment Equations", Review of Economic Studies, 58: pp. 277-297.

Arellano, Manuel and Olympia Bover. 1995. "Another Look at the Instrumental Variables Estimation of Error Component Models", Journal of Econometrics, 68: pp. 29-52.

Azam, Jean-Paul., Augustin Fosu, and Njugana S. Ndung'u. 2002. "Explaining Slow Growth in Africa", African Development Review, 14: pp. 177- 220.

Abdou Moumouni. 1968. "Education in Africa", 1st American Edition

Chinua, Achebe. 1958. Things Fall Apart, Anchor Books, a division of Freedom House Inc. New York

Babatunde, Adetunji Musibau. 2006. "Trade Policy Reform, Regional Integration and Export Performance in the ECOWAS Sub-Region", Working Paper, Department of Economics, University of Ibadan, Ibadan Nigeria.

Balogun, Emmanuel Dele. 2008. "An Alternative Reconsideration of Macroeconomic Convergence Criteria for West African Monetary Zone", MPRA Working Paper No. 11367, University of Munich, Munich Germany.

Barro, Robert J. 1991. "Economic Growth in a Cross Section of Countries", Quarterly Journal of Economics, 106: pp. 407-443.

Boivin, Jean., Marc P. Giannoni and Benoit Mojon. 2008. "How Has the Euro Changed the Monetary Transmission?" Working Paper 14190, National Bureau of Economic Research, Cambridge, MA.

Byrne, Joseph P., Julia Darby and Ronald MacDonald. 2008. "U.S Trade and Exchange Rate Volatility: A Real Sectoral Bilateral Analysis", Journal of Macroeconomics, 30: pp. 238-259.

Cameron, Colin A., Jonah B. Gelbach and Douglas L. Miller. 2007. "Bootstrap-Based Improvements for Inference with Clustered Errors", Technical Working Paper 344, National Bureau of Economic Research, Cambridge, MA.

Debrun, Xavier, Masson, Paul. and Catherine Pattillo. 2003. "West African Currency Union Rationale and Sustainability", CESifo Economic Studies, 49: pp. 381-413.

Dixit, Avinash. 2000. "A Repeated Game Model of Monetary Union" Economic Journal, 110: pp. 759-780.

Dore, Mohammed H.I. 1993. The Macro dynamics of Business Cycles: A Comparative Evaluation, Blackwell Publishers, Cambridge, MA

Durlauf, Steven N., Andros Kourtellos and Artur Minkin. 2001. "The Local Solow Growth Model", European Economic Review, 45: pp. 928-940. Easterly,

Willliam and Richard Levine. 1997. "Africa's Growth Tragedy: Policies and Ethnic Divisions", Quarterly Journal of Economics, 113: pp. 1203-1250.

Elu, Juliet. 1998. "ECOWAS and Economic Integration in West Africa", Journal of African Finance and Economic Development, 3: pp. 149-169.

Fosu, Augustin K. 2008. "Democracy and Growth in Africa: Implications of Increasing Electoral Competitiveness", Economics Letters, 100: pp. 442- 444.

Frankel, Jeffrey A. and Andrew K. Rose. 1998. "The Endogeneity of the Optimum Currency Area Criteria", Economic Journal, 108: pp. 1009- 1025.

Geda, Alemayehu and Haile Kebret. 2007. "Regional Economic Integration in Africa: A Review of Problems and Prospects with a Case Study of COMESA", Journal of African Economies, 17: pp. 357-394.

Greene, William H. 2003. Econometric Analysis, 5th Edition, Prentice Hall, Upper Saddle River, NJ

UGyimah-Brempong, Kwabena and Marva E. Corley. 2005. "Civil Wars and Economic Growth in Sub-Saharan Africa", Journal of African Economies, 14: pp. 270-311.

Hannik, Dean M. and J. Henry Owusu. 1998. "Has ECOWAS Promoted Trade Among Its Members?" Journal of African Economies, 7: pp. 363- 383,

Hausman, Jerry A., and William E. Taylor. 1981. "Panel Data and Unobservable Individual Effects", Econometrica, 49: pp. 1377-1398.

Huber, Peter J. 1967. "The Behavior of Maximum Likelihood Estimates under Nonstandard Conditions," Proceedings of the Fifth Berkeley Symposium on Mathematical Statistics and Probability, 1: pp. 221-233.

Irving, Jacqueline. 1999. "For Better or For Worse: The Euro and the CFA Franc", Africa Recovery, United Nations Department of Information, 12: pp. 24-29.

Islam, Nazrul. 1995. "Growth Empirics: A Panel Data Approach", Quarterly Journal of Economics, 110: pp. 1127-1170.

Kaldor, Nicholas. 1961. "Capital Accumulation and Economic Growth", in the Theory of Capital, (eds.)

Friedrich A. Lutz and Douglas C. Hague, pp. 177-222, Macmillan, London, UK.

Lee, Kevin., M. Hashem Pesaran, and Ron Smith. 1998. "Growth Empirics: A Panel Data Approach---A Comment", Quarterly Journal of Economics, 113: pp. 319-323.

Mankiw, Gregory, N., David Romer, and David N. Weil. 1992. "A Contribution To The Empirics Of Economic Growth", Quarterly Journal of Economics, 107: pp. 407-437.

Masson, Paul R. 2008. "Currency Unions in West Africa: Is the Trade Effect Substantial Enough to Justify Their Formation?", World Economy, 31: pp. 533-547.

McCallum, Bennett T. 1989. "Real Business Cycle Models", in Modern Business Cycle Theory, Robert J. Barro, (Ed.) Harvard University Press, Cambridge, MA.

McKinnon, Ronald. 1963. "Optimum Currency Areas", American Economic Review, 52: pp. 717-725.

Muhammad, Andrew. 2009. "Would African Countries Benefit from the Termination of Kenya's Economic Partnership Agreement (EPA) with the EU? An Analysis of EU Demand for Imported Roses", Journal of Agricultural Economics, 60: pp. 220-238.

Otonti Nduka. 1964. Education and the Nigerian Cultural Background. Oxford University Pres. England

Okada, Toshiro. 2006. "What Does The Solow Model Tell Us About Economic Growth?" Contributions to Macroeconomics, 6: pp. 1-30.

Papp, Richard. Philip Hans Franses, and Dick Van Dijk. 2005. "Does Africa Grow Slower than Asia, Latin America, and the Middle East?: Evidence from a New Data-based Classification Method", Journal of Development Economics, 77: pp. 553-570.pper Saddle River, N J

Walter, Rodney. 1973. How Europe Underdeveloped Africa, Howard University Press, Washington, DC

www.blackstarnews.com/.../eurozone-crisis-global-recession-and-the-future of the f.CFA...

Apr 16, 2012 - Who: Salomon Samen, Ph.D., Economist and **Nash Kpokou, Ph.D.**, Consultant & Economist

www.ivoirebusiness.net/?q.../**nash-kpokou-phd**...May 9, 2012 - **Nash Kpokou, Ph.D** Economist & International Business Consultant: Après la chute spectaculaire de Sarkozy, les Militants du RDR récusent le gouvernememt Ouattara

Mar 22, 2011 - Les Banques Coloniales Françaises en Cote d'Ivoire et le Terrorisme Bancaire de **Nash Kpokou, Ph.D** | mardi 22 mars 2011 ... **nashkpokouphd**.blogspot.com/

Jan 5, 2011 LE F. CFA ET L'ESCLAVAGE MONÉTAIRE EN AFRIQUE FRANCOPHONE-par **Nash Kpokou** ... **Ph.D** Économiste & International Business Consultant. Nouvelles - Afrique-Mondewww. afriquemonde.org/index1.php

Juillet 2. 2011. LA NOUVELLE MONNAIE ET L'OPINION PUBLIQUE IVOIRIEN, par Nash Kpokou, Ph.D. news.abidjan.net/h/403305.html

Juin 19, 2012. VERITE CHOQUANTE SUR LE CHOMAGE EN COTE D'IVOIRE QUE OUATTARA CACHE AUX IVOIRIENS par Nash Kpokou, Ph.D .www.africaview.net

Janvier 25, 2011. LA BANQUE CENTRALE DE LA COTE D'IVOIRE ET LA CONVERTIBILITE DE LA NOUVELLE MONNAIE IVOIRIENNE par Nash Kpokou, Ph.D .www.fr.icom7.com

Apr 20, 2013. QUELLE ELECTION DANS LE DESORDRE ET L INSECURITE AVEC DES PROMESSES ELECTORALES FARFELUES, par Nash Kpokou, Ph.D. www.afrikinfos.com

Jan 5, 2011. LA NOUVELLE MONNAIE IVOIRIENNE., par Nash Kpokou. www.news.abidjan.net•

Feb 15, 2013. **BLING BLING ECONOMIQUE ET PAUVRETE EN COTE D'IVOIRE, par Nash Kpokou, Ph.D. www.afriquemonde.org**

Oct 2, 2013. LES PERFORMANCES ECONOMIQUES DU PRESIDENT GBAGBO POUR LA COTE D'IVOIRE, par Nash Kpokou, Ph.D. www.gbosahoua.gbodosahoua. Blogspot, com

Yunus, Muhammad (1999). Banker to the Poor (first ed). United States. Public Affairs

Yunus, Muhammad (2007). Creating a World Without poverty: Social Business and the Future of Capitalism, United States: Public Affairs

Joseph E. Stiglitz (2002). Globalization and Its Discontents, WW Norton & Company, New York

Thomas, Sowell (2012). TrIckle Down THEORY AND tax Cuts for the Rich. Hoover Institution Press, 1st edition. United States

INDEX

Printed in the United States
By Bookmasters